Don't Go Near The Water

British Petroleum and Alaska Workers' Compensation Division Practices Exposed

Mervyn Eggleston

Publication Consultants
Since 1978

PO Box 221974 Anchorage, Alaska 99522-1974
books@publicationconsultants.com
www.publicationconsultants.com

ISBN 978-1-59433-133-6
eBook 978-1-59433-140-4
Library of Congress Catalog Card Number: 2010902146

Manufactured in the United States of America.

Dedication

Dedicated to innocent people who have suffered because of those who do not understand fair play.

Contents

Chapter One
A Long Hot Summer

It was hot in Arkansas during the summer of 1993 for a fifty-five-year-old man working long, hard hours with a bunch of kids in their twenties, on crews that were framing houses. The heat probably seemed worse to me than to the locals, too. Years of living in Alaska had made me into a person who doesn't do well when it gets much above seventy. There was a reason for my being here or even in the South-48 at all. (That's what Alaskans call the unfortunate part of America that isn't in Alaska.) As far as Arkansas was concerned, it was purely about economics. There would turn out to be more to that side of things than I might have expected.

One fellow I worked with, Charlie, was amazing to me. He worked on high roofs, moved huge stacks of lumber by hand and endured long and very hard hours. Probably more, he fought the financial climate of a very low-end business. We were near the bottom of the food chain, often ending up with less than what a minimum-wage job might have paid. Work had to be bid for and that was very competitive. Help was usually made up of guys who were more or less unemployable elsewhere or who were just doing this while they looked for better work.

In Northwestern Arkansas the Wal-Mart boom had made some people rich. One old farmer knew his hay fields would be turning into subdivisions but was too old to do much with it himself. His grandson fell into a deal he couldn't refuse. The kid became a developer, hiring houses built on his grandparents' property. He had a huge home on the lake and drove a fancy car. One day he told me, "These framers are too greedy, I can bring in Mexicans." Such was the way of the real world I was seeing.

Clyde worked for Charlie. At one time he had been better employed. His former job had been on an oil field in one of the western states. There had been an accident with an on-the-job injury. I never did find out what happened. "I used to think of our manager as a friend," he told me once. Feeling bad because of being hurt on the job, he was told "Don't worry about this; it's why we pay for insurance." For all of that, and even his position on the job, Clyde found himself out on his ear and was sour on big companies. He didn't say much about it but did say something once that I remember. "I had it all," he said, "wife and baby, new house and new car, too." Clyde had had a good position with his company. Being the kind of worker he was, it probably had to be that way. He had thought of all of it as being something special.

This man had a big old Plymouth station wagon, which was where he slept. Some friends lived about thirty miles away. He either bathed at their place or went swimming. Some young police officers used to like to pull through the subdivisions at night and wake him up. Sometimes they did it more than once a night. It was hot out there, too. I used to wonder how he could stand it but there didn't seem to be much choice for him.

His teeth were so bad that it really showed. For him, a trip to the dentist would have been as unrealistic as a personal tour of Buckingham Palace.

One day Clyde said "You don't smoke but you cough and gag a lot, why is that?" Then, without hesitating, he said "Don't tell me, let me guess. They had an air compressor hooked up to the water system where you worked; right?"

His comment startled me. The question had to be asked. "How did you know?"

Bushy hair, jagged teeth and all, a sunburned little guy who looked as if he didn't even have a life looked up at me and grinned. "Heck," he said, "everybody knows you can't pressure up a water system on an oil rig with an air compressor. You'll make someone sick."

The next day he came in to work and spoke to me. "I went down to my friends' place last night," he said. "When I told them about what had happened to you they couldn't believe it. Those big Alaskan companies are supposed to be the pros." It turned out that Clyde's friends were from the same oil field he was. Apparently, *everyone* knew about something that had touched my life in a big way because I wasn't in on the secret. Clyde had hit the nail right on the head.

There is a story here and I believe it really does need to be told, for a lot of people's sakes. It is several years old and continues to age. Over time, it has been written about once in a while. Nothing has ever come of it. An unknown person with no money and a lot of opposition from well-placed people can't go very far. As this has been written and then rewritten, over and over, entries lose continuity. A comment from one year might show up sandwiched into when another was being written or rewritten. Still, this is important and I keep trying to get the story out.

Here, as this is being re-written again, I make a decision. That is to use real names where I believe a person, acting in the course of their particular capacity, had a part (perhaps even just a very small one) in what took place; it is more about the capacity, than the person. To me, the matter is incredibly significant but a particular person's contribution to it might not be overwhelming; probably-to-certainly not conscious. I believe that most people are of good intention. No reflection on anyone's character is intended. I am not accusing anyone of anything more serious, here, than human nature.

Chapter Two
A Strange Situation

In January 1976 I went to work for B.P. Alaska. That is to say British Petroleum, doing business in Alaska. The job was on the oil field at Prudhoe Bay, on what is called the *North Slope*. It is usually just called *The Slope*. That's where the land slopes gradually northward, toward the Beaufort Sea. The job paid very well and there was a feeling of being a part of something special. I had been a power plant operator for around fifteen years at the time, working at doing that in a lot of places. For five years or so I had been away from the power business, having a go at building houses. It felt really good to be where I was and back to doing what I had done for years.

The place reminded me of when I had been in Greenland but conditions were great and home was only a few hours away. Work was a week of twelve-hour shifts followed by a week off duty, at home. That meant a lot of flying and I loved all of it.

Although my memory of timing is vague, something new came along during the first year or so. This was pain. It was inside me and it was terrible. When it happened I could only hold on and hurt. Then it would go away, to return whenever it wanted to. That could be anytime and there didn't seem to be a pattern to it. Nothing had ever gone wrong with me before except when I'd had my appendix out nearly twenty years before. I tried to ignore this and think, now, that I was afraid of it and was in denial. Over time, both the frequency and intensity of the pain diminished but it still hurt badly when it came on. I believe that some things happened to me back then. A condition developed that is hard to explain. Over the next few years it worsened.

In the spring of 1979 another mysterious thing happened. I had been with the company for a little more than three years. One night I found myself waking up in agony. I still felt the original problem at times but this was completely different. There is no way, I believe, the pain could have been worse. It seemed to be in the muscles or where they connected to my bones. Along with the pain there was something strange. That was a very real sensation of coldness. Intense as if I was being burned, it was very cold. When this happened I would run hot water into the bathtub and just lie there and suffer.

Again, this was something that didn't seem to have an apparent reason and I missed work over it. The doctor talked about various things. None of them seemed to actually describe what was taking place. The sensation of coldness stopped when the pain was happening. Gradually, this problem became less excruciating but was still extremely bad.

In the spring of 1981 another weird thing happened. A thick, crusty rash formed on the knuckles of my hands. It itched horribly. In fact, the itch was more like a sting. As thick as scabs, which it closely resembled, this rash seemed like a living thing. It would grow then sort of thin out but it never went away. At times the revolting mess would crack and run a fluid. A spot of rash came onto the calf of my right leg, too. It itched the same way. I finally learned that Hydrocortisone cream would sooth the itch but nothing could be done for the rash. One day, in the break room, I saw one of our guys, Johnny, putting the same cream on his hands. Our rashes were identical. I have never seen this anywhere else.

Gradually, around that time, I started to have to clear my throat a lot. It got to where I was miserable with it and found that it annoyed people. A general loss of awareness and ability began to be noticeable in me. I couldn't explain any of this and it was getting worse. I now had the intense pains, that condition, the rash and the throat clearing. None of it seemed to be related to anything and apparently the problems had nothing to do with each other. I had started to get blisters in my hair, just above my neck, too.

Things would become even stranger. It was after the rash came on that the next thing started. I would fly away every other week for a tour of duty. Afterward, it was home for a week. The complete cycle took two weeks. I began to arrive home with my stomach growling, which would get louder and louder. In public, people have looked up at me from clear across a big room. In a few days there would be a set-to in the bathroom with heavy pressure and much volume. That volume, though, was just clear water. There was no substance, color or odor and no feeling of sickness, either. This was just clear water and lots of it. It happened a few times a day for a two or three days and then things went back to normal. They stayed that way until my next return home from work, exactly two weeks later, with my stomach growling. I could have set my calendar by it.

Gradually the precise timing started to slip and the duration of the problem lengthened. Eventually, the norm for that became anywhere from ten days to three weeks or more. With a week-on – week- off schedule, this meant that it could be happening at any time, in relation to my work. I used to wonder what became of the food I was eating.

Work rocked along for years. So did the problem. This was happening around a third of the time. The very first time it happened I had been given some medication for the pain. It didn't help, nothing ever touched that pain. The medication was stopped right away but it had nothing to do with what was going on. The problem was with me to stay. A doctor asked me if I had been drinking water from any new wells or from streams. That didn't fit. Nothing seemed to explain any of what was going on.

In the break room at work the fellows were talking about something they called the *North Slope Crud*. One of them, George, said that the kitchen people were careless and didn't throw food away when it was old. "They're trying to kill us," he said. I didn't comment because my situation was just too embarrassing. Also, because my diarrhea was so profound and unusual, I didn't associate it with what was being talked about, anyway.

A time came when I began to experience awful pains in my chest area. Often there was heavy heartburn, too. It was so bad that I went to the emergency room once. A doctor had me wearing a device, for a week, which monitored my heart. That had always been strong. A nurse told me I had the blood pressure of a teen-aged boy. Still, the pains and the heartburn got worse and worse.

The doctor who had monitored me was doing her workup. The report was slow in coming and so, finally, I called her. She said that it looked as if I drank too much coffee. In the time and at the place I grew up, coffee and tea were off limits to kids. That didn't matter, I wasn't even curious. To me, even today, they both smell bad. The doctor was told that I didn't use either of them. We went through pop with caffeine in it, which I do not use, and then cocoa; ditto. The pains continued without explanation.

The power-plant was bigger and more modern than any other place was where I had worked before and I had been away from this field for awhile, too. However, in the trade, most plants are different. It usually takes time to "break in." Beyond all of that, though, there was something I couldn't account for and it went on and on and got worse with time. Confusion and even disorientation came easily. It could be hard to sort things out. At times there could even be what seemed to be moodiness, which is alien to me.

This situation became more and more noticeable. Finally some very strange things began to happen. One of those took place at camp; Base Operations Center (BOC) where our living quarters and the company's on-slope offices were. I saw a man, shook hands with him and spoke of a matter we both knew about. He just stared at me. This was not who I thought it was and he and I had known each other for years, too. There wasn't even a resemblance. At times, my thoughts seemed to be spliced together like film clips.

Driving up the Alaska Highway in 1983, we came over a hill and there was the ocean. Then I realized that this was the middle of the Yukon and there could be no ocean. The world rolled over then, and the sky went back up to where it belonged. I pulled over.

Chapter Three
Life With The Problem

George was working out in the plant. He was late getting back to the control area but had not finished his work. Something had happened to him. He kept putting his hand to his face in trying to describe it. He was off work for quite a while after that. There was talk on the crew of mental problems for him.

In March, 1989, five of my children and I were driving through Canada on our way to the South-48. It was during one of the long problem times that I'd been having. The situation had been with me, without explanation, for more than seven years by then. Early in the morning we were parked and sleeping, in a pull-off. I woke up and looked around. My seventeen-year-old was in the passenger side recliner. I thought he could spell me later, driving. We started out but then, somehow, were sitting along the road.

My son spoke to me quietly, saying, "Dad, are you alright?"

Something felt very strange. There was a moment of trying to get things sorted out. It didn't work. "I'm confused," I said.

The reply was a quiet "I guess you are."

There was a slightly sickish feeling and things still weren't working. Unhooking my seat belt, I opened the door, stepped out onto the highway, and fell flat on my face. The boys came around the van and helped me up. I staggered, with their help, away from the traffic side. They leaned me up with my back against the van. The fall was headlong and face down, into a ditch full of snow.

The kids picked me up again, opened the big side door and laid me on my back in the van. One of the girls had a piece of hard candy. She had heard that when a person acted like this they might need sugar and pushed the candy into my mouth. Afraid of choking, I managed to push it out with my tongue. After that, I don't remember the sequence of events. Convulsions came on and I wretched and bounced. It hurt and I had a terrible feeling of being completely helpless. Either before or after that I was talking to the kids. We were hundreds of miles from home, in a foreign country. I was trying to tell them where our money was. Cash was in my billfold but we had traveler's checks, too. There was only a very little voice and not much power to get it out. I was fading.

I heard my oldest boy yelling, out on the highway. He had stopped a truck. After that I was sort of aware but very weak and sick. My son was driving, following a truck driven by someone who knew the area and the way to a hospital. People in white came running out of a doorway. They took me into the emergency room. I was badly dehydrated.

Things started to come back into focus in a hospital bed with an I.V. in my arm. It was then, that my kids told me quite a story. My son had heard me speak, though I don't remember saying anything, but continued to doze. As we were under-way he opened an eye and then both. I was unconscious and the van was in on-coming traffic, on cruise control at highway speed. My son fought the wheel over my limp body. Cars went off the road and into the snow, with their horns blaring. It was a van load of scared kids. I don't remember any of it.

Back home, I went to see my doctor. This was a man some people said wasn't very good at what he did. I had come to him, as a patient, when he bought my old doctor's practice. As for me, I noticed the papers on his wall and saw that he had been an officer at a well-known air force hospital. I had been an airman and that settled it for me. I figured that the old timers in a little town were just not willing to give a new guy a chance. He decided to send me up to Anchorage, to someone more specialized.

The people in Anchorage went clear through me. There didn't seem to be anything that could account for the problem. This specialist asked me if I been drinking water from questionable sources.

The answer was what it had always been. One thing came out of this that I had heard before, too. It was what I had been told in Canada. I needed to drink at least eight glasses of water a day. This was especially true, I was told, when the *clear water* problem was underway.

The paper cups in our break room were 12 ounces each. Eight of those would be a lot of water. Along with that, one thing was apparent. The water at the plant tasted a little bit strange. Before I got there the fellows had put in their own filter and faucet, in order to make coffee. Some of them said they wouldn't drink our water. The cooler kept it cold, though. That made a difference.

Our foreman, Jay, got me a big bottle of lemon juice from the kitchen. One little cap full went into each cup. It made the water seem to taste better. The guys on the crew would say, "That stuff tastes terrible, how can you drink it?" One of them said he had seen inside the water pipes and there was a "snotty white substance in them." I didn't really believe much of that. The company had one of the best water treatment plants in the industry. There was a lot of publicity about it when the oil field was coming on line.

I just thought the water tasted that way because the water was stored in a steel tank and ran through steel pipes. The whole power-plant was made of steel; even the floors. Water didn't taste like that anywhere else.

Chapter Four
The CPS Water System

B.P. has a big lake at its North-Slope operations, which has been enlarged and lined. This is where the water comes from. It passes through a state-of-the art treatment plant and goes out to the various facilities by truck. Each of those facilities has a big tank, called a receiver, and a small pressure tank and pump like the ones a person might use with a well.

Our plant, the Central Power Station (CPS), was different. There, we had the big tank but no pump or pressure tank. Whoever built the place had just piped air to the receiver, from the compressed air system. The compressed air was stored in a tank the same size as our water tank and they sat side-by-side. Both are listed at 2,200 gallons but we always said 1,800. Either way, that's a lot of air. It was used in two ways. One air outlet pipe went into a system where the air was filtered and dried. Called instrument air, it was used for sensitive pneumatic applications. The rest was called service air. It was just raw air. That was what pressured the water system.

The water tank was re-filled every other day. Our people closed the valve the tank was pressurized through. Then they opened another valve, at the top, venting the tank's pressure. After this, the intake valve was opened and water was pumped in from a truck, outside. The tank was vertical, five feet in diameter and about fifteen feet tall. Water came into it at the top, under pressure, and fell into whatever was left from the last time we filled up. Usually, that was from five-to-eight hundred gallons.

Delivery pressure was such that it gave us around a thousand gallons in fifteen to twenty minutes. We *took on water* every other day.

The water system was modified in 1987. I vaguely recall hearing that the tank, as a pressure vessel, was one of many such vessels owned by the company. Those had to be routinely tested and recertified by the State. This was both an inconvenience and an expense. The change was to atmospheric pressure and the tank was no longer pressurized. The valve at the top was left open and we had a pressure tank and pump, like everyone else did. The old air line was left in place, though. This was so that we could use pressurized air to blow the remaining water out of the fill line to prevent it from freezing. The tank would be filled and pressurized like it had been before the change. That pressure was sent out through the fill line and the whole thing was left at atmospheric pressure until the next fill-up.

I wasn't involved in the change but found out that it included an automatic bleeder system, to keep moisture from accumulating in the air tank, and some new filters. Those were supposed to be the very best; charcoal filters. These might be interesting changes, I now suppose, for a project that was just meant to do away with a pressure vessel. Also, at the time, I didn't even think about the fact that the tank was opened and cleaned out. The system was down for a few days.

There was a time when the company sent teams of people on *fact-finding* missions. It was November, 1990. This was around twenty months after I had lost consciousness behind the wheel. On the plane coming into St. Louis, I felt a sore throat coming on. There had been a lot of those in recent years and I always had a roll of throat lozenges in my briefcase. Only one, that I could find, was strong enough to help me. The lozenges, Hydrocortisone cream for my rash, and some Tums for the heartburn were things I could not do without. On this trip, though, I had no briefcase. It was an oversight that would be regretted.

My travels had taken me to Florida. As the sore throat got worse and worse, I looked for those lozenges in vain. Druggists told me that there are different regulations in different states. The stuff I used was too strong to be sold over the counter in Florida. This would be nine days of the worst sore throat I have ever had—before or since. When it was over there was a sore spot down in my throat. It became worse with time.

Chapter Five
The Plot Thickens

Our water had started to be very bad. It was a gradual thing, going from mildly *off* to distasteful and then to having a definite harsh taste and foul smell. Those became stronger and stronger. This had happened about nine months before, too. The water department, Central Water Treatment Facility (CWTF), took samples of our water every other week. They tested for various things but not, as it worked out, for what was going bad in the water they were testing, which would have been completely unexpected. That first time they did not know of the problem. They tested over and over while the water just got worse and worse.

The guys kept getting after the boss. Jay always said the water was okay and that it was treated better here than it would have been anywhere else. Mostly, he drank Pepsi. At one point, he had one of our big plastic sample bottles and would bring it to work, full of pop. We were the two men on the crew who did not drink coffee. His intake of water seemed to be very limited, at least to the point where he wasn't aware of the problem. He didn't humor the fellows who were aware of it, either.

It finally got bad enough and the guys complained enough, though, that he called the water department. One of their people came to the power plant. He took a paper cup from the break room and got some water from the fountain. "Whew," he said, "this is some bad stuff." The tank was drained and refilled with super-chlorinated water. That sat for twenty four hours and was drained and refilled.

That had been months ago. This time it was worse. Our crew grumped at Jay. He did like he had the last time. "The water is fine, he would say. It just got worse and worse, as the water people did their testing (but apparently, not their tasting) and he drank his Pepsi.

A group of men worked out of the power plant. One of their guys tried to take a drink from the cooler and said "Yuk, this stuff tastes just like oil." It smelled like oil, too. I remember thinking that it wasn't the first time, either.

Their man called into the office and Jay came out. He bent over the cooler and tried to take a drink. Then he said "You get your repair," and went to the phone. Again, this was a time when he didn't seem to have known about the problem even though the men had griped to him about it for weeks. It was another time, too, when the water department didn't know about it even though they had tested the water constantly.

It was the first week of January, 1991. My forced water drinking had gone on since April, 1989. That was done through one siege of bad taste and its repair. It had continued to near-the- top of another escalation. Assurances from Jay and the blessings of bottled lemon juice had made it possible. The taste had become so bad that I couldn't drink the water at all.

A different man from the water department came this time. Henry had a lot of experience in the water treatment field. The same things were done as had been done the time before but with a few differences. The water filters that had been installed in 1987 were taken out and replaced with a different kind. Also, there was a surprise. Henry told Jay, "We can't serve you water because there is an air line between your water tank and the plant's air system. That's a cross connection and is against code."

Jay explained that we had to have the air line to blow out the intake, to keep it from freezing. Henry said, "I'm sorry but you'll have to rework that situation." The discussion continued but I could see who was going to win. I went back to the mechanical room and got some wrenches. Jay came in, and together, we got the job done. That air line was history. What I noticed most was the very good taste of the water after this repair and cleaning.

At the time, my stomach was in the growling stages of the approaching problem, which was then more than nine years old. It came, was relatively short and has never offered to come back. That was eighteen years ago. It had slowed in recent years but was harder to handle when it did come on. Soon, another thing went away. That awful rash on my knuckles disappeared and has never offered to come back, either. It took a few months to start to suspect what had happened. Even then, though, I had doubts. It all seemed just too big to be real.

At home, I shared my thoughts with my wife. The biggest problem did seem to be gone but she was skeptical. Nearly ten years is a long time for some profound thing to exist, just to have it just go away suddenly. "Let's see your hands," she said. I held them out. The rash was completely gone.

In trying to get things sorted out, I called a doctor. He told me I probably should call the Alaska Department of Environmental Conservation (ADEC), they were the experts on water. That was done and my call got passed around until it came to someone who seemed to know what he was talking about. This man spoke of microscopic organisms. He said that some of them can live in a chlorine environment. According to him they can be some "tough customers." If there is the right kind of contamination they have food. "If you get a feeding cycle going," he said, "you can have real trouble. They can form colonies."

Around this time I made a trip to the South-48. Visiting an aunt, I told her what was going on and about my suspicions. She looked suddenly serious. "Mervyn," she said, "Please listen to what I'm going to tell you. I know how you feel about that job and what you think of those people but, believe me, they are not your friends. If they get a doctor, you get a doctor and you get a lawyer." She went on to tell me that when my uncle was alive he had known a man who worked for the Union Pacific Railroad. Something had happened and he fell into the hands of the managers and their attorneys. I remember her comment well. "I don't know why they don't have the same ethics as the rest of us but they don't."

That business about lawyers reminds me. I never thought I'd ever need one. In the fifties, stationed at an air force base in California, some friends and I were driving into San Jose when a truck hit us from behind. I was cut up a little bit but one of the guys was hurt. In a week or so I got a call to come down to the main gate. A civilian down there wanted to talk to me. He was a lawyer. I was told that since the truck had hit us from behind, they would have to pay. This fellow commented about what seemed like a lot of money, telling me his fee would be a percentage and if there was no settlement there would be no cost. I was offended and told him to take a hike.

Where possible effects of the water were concerned, the man at ADEC told me I should probably call the Center for Disease Control. A fellow there said he would look into it and get back to me.

Chapter Six
The World We Live In

Things had been happening to me that I didn't tell anyone about. I began to wonder about the guys on the crew and, in the break room, a few of them were told about the clear water diarrhea. The man who had said there was a snotty white substance in the water pipes had once been in management of a big company. He said that if I reported this it would cost me my job. Another said I'd be throwing my friends to the wolves. Then the guys tore into the H.R. people. What they had to say was surprising to me and very derogatory. This was all wearing thin with me. In the first place it was not my way. In the second, I didn't believe it at all. To me, the company was as professional as anyone could ever be. Along with this, we were supposed to report safety problems. That had been drummed into us and made sense to me. Failure to do so could result in discipline up to and including dismissal. I was surprised to hear guys of their caliber talking this way.

It was May, 1991. At the office, Larry Motz was on duty. He and I had been working for the company about the same length of time. For me, that was a little bit more than fifteen years. Although we were not well acquainted we did talk, even kidding around. I had introduced him to my wife, once, when we met in town. His brother was principal of a school and I was on the parents' advisory council to the school board. My feelings toward both men were of respect.

Larry had once told me that I was "respected here." He was probably the best person for me to talk to about the water problem. Even knowing him, though, this was embarrassing. I asked if it could be kept as quiet as possible.

"We can't do that," he said, "the exposure is too great. Think about how many people have drunk the water there."

I was told to put what I had reported to him into writing. The next day, when I was turning that in, I saw a notice on his bulletin board. It was one of those government things few people notice and even fewer understand. It said something about a form and I asked him about it. He told me (I allege) that I could fill out a form if I wanted to but it wasn't necessary because I had reported it to him in writing. It was just one more thing I didn't understand, which didn't have to be bothered with.

Very soon a memo came to me acknowledging my report. Within just a few days, something else came from HR. This was the C.P.S. Water Quality Report. Even with the very limited understanding I had some interesting things could be seen. The report was totally one way. Also, it wasn't very accurate. According to what I read, our water was excellent and the water department was on top of everything. My situation was distanced from the water system.

This was from the industrial hygienist, Allen Gillie. It was in 2008, while I was rewriting this for the umpteenth time, that a light came on for me. The report was ostensibly from Gillie but the information in it was from the water plant supervisor, Jim O'Niel. Apparently he had put on a presentation. Today, I cannot even imagine an industrial hygienist who would endorse the water system we had and am not surprised that Gillie made essentially no input to what was alleged to be his department's report. At last and finally, I think that something interesting was happening here, early-on.

The whole thing was a downer. There had been years of bizarre situations. Then there had been a sudden and mysterious resolution of some of them. Now I sat looking at a rather strange report and wondering. No doubt about it; there were things in the report that were wrong. My personal knowledge, as limited as it was, told me that. Still, these were the pros. Even if some things were out of order, the overall scenario might have been roughly as they were saying.

To me, the water problem was an important matter that was being addressed by sincere, competent professionals. A letter was written to them. In it, I discussed the report. There was a lot to comment about. Jim had said that his people tested routinely. When problems were detected because of water being tanked storage, his group did a clean-up. There seemed to be some misunderstanding here. I had seen, twice, how our water's problems had gone undetected for weeks. The call for repair came from us both times. This was not just about water going stale, either, the taste and even the smell had been terrible. With usage of several hundred gallons per day and a constant re-filling, "tanked storage" would hardly have applied.

The report said there was nothing unusual about the cleanup of the CPS water system. No mention was made of that strong harsh taste, the smell, or even of the other clean-up about nine months before. There was no mention, either, of the super clean-up about six years earlier, when the company did away with a "pressure vessel." That time, the tank was actually opened and cleaned out. The report went on and on. There was much to see but I knew so little about any of this that most of it just went over my head.

This report said the change to atmospheric pressure was ordered by the water department and was for the purpose of decreasing, "by one," the number of pressure vessels requiring certification. That was what I vaguely remembered having heard.

There was no answer from the office and there never would be. Once, in the camp, Larry told me "Slow down, come to a school zone." It came to me that all of this needed to be looked into further. Some questions needed to be answered. Those answers could be about the water or they might turn out to be about something else. It all seemed serious at the time.

In his report, O'Niel said some interesting things. He had gone to water treatment school in California. Apparently they had a system that was like ours. As a part of being away from home so much we had use of the long-distance lines. Our access phones were in the lobby, at camp. Off duty, I called the school. A man told me that he'd been there since the fifties. He said the school had been on public water the whole time. I described the system at work to him. He said it sounded as if it might be a cross connection (potential source of contamination) and could be illegal.

He referred me to another man, who talked about something called a cushion tank. This was not really like what we had and would not be allowed in a public water system. They are used for irrigation, though. This man said that his own father had one on his farm.

O'Niel's next example was at Ft. Wainwright, near Fairbanks. He had worked there in a water treatment plant. Apparently, here was a system in point. I made another call. At that place a person spoke to me who had been there for a few years. He said there was a new plant and that the old one, which had been built in the forties, had been torn down in the seventies. According to him there were things in that old plant, which would never be allowed today.

"Why," he said, "they even had a cushion tank in there." When I described our system he said it sounded like a cross connection to him and that he would call the ADEC. I called them and a man said he would come to *The Slope* and look into it.

Chapter Seven
How To Mess Up Water

I found out a lot while I was calling around and would continue to do that for some time. What was learned can be given here. The practice of pressurizing a water system from an air compressor is a downer. Being a cross connection, it is also illegal. The first problem is the air itself. Clean air, under most conditions, is rare at best. However, unless a person wants to live in a bubble there isn't much that can or needs to be done about it; but do not put air into drinking water. There can be dirt, mold, germs, and other microorganisms in it and the water can become their medium.

Compressors add a sort of spin to all of this. They take a piece of air, with all that it may contain, and stuff it into a little space. Then they grab some more and shove it in there, too. The process is repeated again and again. The result is that many volumes of air are in a space which would not normally hold them. A cubic foot of compressed air holds the contents of several cubic feet of air at atmospheric pressure.

To this we can add something that isn't usually in the air; oil vapor. Mechanical parts have to be lubricated. This calls for oil on the cylinder walls, to prevent friction, which ends up in the outgoing air. Even the finest conventional compressor, in the very best condition, cannot help but to move oil vapor, as well as whatever else the air might have contained to begin with. Any such compressor can cause trouble, but one that is worn out could be a source of disaster.

There is more to consider. Modern oils contain additives and those are in the mix. Some changes to the oil are had because of heat in the compressor head. These could be about possible varnishes and so forth. That heat probably helps to lighten and vaporize the oil, too. Crankcase oil is not clean oil, either. There is nothing good about any of this. Whatever is involved in lubricating a compressor is in the air it produces.

Another significant part of this is moisture. Air lines are hot and generate a certain amount of condensation. This runs in systems that are affected by rust, oil, and air contamination. Also involved, are such microorganisms as might get along with all of this. Those things are why divers cannot use just any air. The wrong stuff could poison them. Professionals realize that there are things in water that can hurt people, even without an air compressor. This is why chlorine has become a part of public water service.

Microscopic organisms behave differently in water than in just air and some of them can live in chlorine. They won't usually be around for long, though, and with nothing to eat... Whatever might be a food source in the water changes the whole picture. These guys can make themselves at home, reproduce, and even form colonies. That's one of the places where oil can have an effect. It's an organic and for these little guys, it is great food. Chlorine didn't hurt them and now it helps them. Like soap, in a way, this cuts the oil and breaks it down. The sludge is reduced to finer particles and dispersed throughout the medium. Suspended in the water, like the stuff in dirty dishwater, all of this forms a rather unfortunate concoction. Oil and oily sludge are bad enough if you have to drink them but the life forms that they support can be bad, too.

The next part of this is a mixture, literally. When some companies make certain chemicals they use what is called a cracker. Petroleum and chlorine are put into a big tank, which is then pressurized and heated. The process is exposed to light. Resulting are various chemicals, called chlorinated hydrocarbons. They include solvents, poisons, and so forth. Our water tank would have made a poor cracker at best but, as I gained understanding, I saw that it was cracker enough to have an effect.

It would be a few years before I reviewed some notes that had been made early on, when I was talking to one of the experts. Short-chain hydrocarbons pass through a person's system faster than long-chain hydrocarbons.

Chapter Eight
Professionals

A letter came in from the Center for Disease Control. Their man spoke of microscopic organisms. He said that if there was a petroleum problem of significance there would be film on the water. I had seen that but it was only out in the plant and years before. We used five-gallon buckets of water for cleanup and for the humidifiers, before water was piped to them. Sheen, as it is called (shiny oily film), was usually on that water; especially after it had set for awhile. I used to look up at the high ceilings where the water pipes ran and wonder why the insides of them were so dirty. I forwarded a copy of the letter to Larry Motz.

The sore down in my throat came to be more and more of a problem and I had to see an ear nose and throat doctor. He found a small lesion on my vocal chords, which would have to be removed. Thoughts came to me about how all of these things were so varied and had gone on for such a long time. The matter appeared to be broader than just a lesion on my vocal chords. I made a decision to find better and more complete services than were available in Alaska. The one I had heard of most was Virginia Mason Clinic, in Seattle. A lot of Alaskans went there.

In those days I still thought that our people were interested and concerned. This was, in my mind, a company matter. We were (I was) still "discussing" the water report. I called Larry and asked if the company would be willing to send me to Seattle so that we could find out what was going on. He replied that such things were up to the company doctor, Jennifer Christian, in Anchorage. I sent her a letter describing what had happened and what my symptoms were.

This was someone I had never met. I called the office in town, in an effort to locate her. The person on the phone said that the doctor was not around. This lady told me she knew of my situation and that it was a personal, non company matter. It felt odd to have a stranger in the Anchorage office know of my situation and I wondered what was happening. On another try, a young-sounding woman told me that Dr. Christian was a great lady. She still wasn't around, though. Finally, on the third try, I connected.

The doctor said that she had not had time to read my letter and was going to be out of town for two weeks, so she wouldn't be able to get to it for a while, either. Then it came. I got chewed out.

"Things happen to people," she said, "When they do we should be prepared to pay for them; that's why we have insurance." If I wanted for her to say this was a company problem, she said, she "would be reluctant to do that. Low-level contamination has been around for years and it doesn't seem to have hurt anyone yet."

Her comments went on for a few minutes and she said "I'll be blunt" at least three times. The water at work had been safe, according to her. It sounded exactly like she was quoting the water report only with an emphasis.

One way or another, I had to do something about the lesion on my vocal chords and that situation called for surgery; which could be done in Alaska or somewhere else. There had been a lot of weird things going on and Virginia Mason did seem like the place to go. This was said to be where people were passed from doctor to doctor, while a complete physical exam was done.

I came into Seattle on the red-eye flight from Anchorage, arriving at the clinic early, and was waiting around the reception area for someone to turn up and tell me where to go. People finally came in and they turned out to be doctors. I was talking to one of them when another one came and butted right in.

"It's reflux" he said. At the time, I had never even heard this term and didn't know what it meant. Then, this doctor told me to stick out my tongue. He went and got a paper towel and, with me still standing in the entry area, wrapped it around my tongue and pulled. That hurt and he didn't seem to see anything.

This was an older man who was a former military officer whose rank had been high. I learned about that while he was talking to me. Dr. Yarrington appeared to still be in charge of everyone else. There were some quiet comments among the other doctors, who seemed to be watching this happen.

The occupational doctors who were a part of Virginia Mason's team were consulted while I was in Seattle. I wouldn't have known that there even was such a thing if Larry hadn't told me, once, that Dr. Christian was the only board certified occupational physician in Alaska. (*Board certified* was another term I hadn't heard before and I didn't know what it meant for awhile, either.) These particular doctors were in a different place than the clinic and I rode on a bus to get there.

In an old run-down building, I found a counter with two men setting behind it. They turned out to be the doctors I was looking for. They were told my story and I offered them a copy of the material that had been furnished to Dr. Christian. One of them stood up and took it. "Let's go into the exam room," he said. Dr. Martin turned out to be interested and thoughtful. He asked a lot of questions as he went over my material. Then he brought up something that wasn't in the material I had brought with me.

"Have you ever had trouble concentrating or focusing your thoughts?" Those problems had become, only too much, a part of my life.

At the clinic a long probe was pushed up my nose and down into whatever is down there. I really didn't know what was going on but this was said to be necessary. That was not a good experience. The probe was with me for twenty four hours and was both slept and showered with it. Removing the thing was a long, drawn-out process, which was really unpleasant. I apologized for having discomfort. The lady who was doing this said I was doing better than a lot of people did. Then she said "the valve is working." I didn't know what that was supposed to mean but knew, from my work, that valves control the flow of fluids and gasses.

A young fellow operated on the lesion with a laser. He seemed to be very skilled but I wasn't going to be awake to find out; they put me to sleep. I found myself waking up on a cot, in a hallway, surrounded by other people who were doing the same. A nurse came by and asked me how I was doing. "Fine," I said, "but I've got to get out of here."

She smiled and said "Why, where are you going?"

When I said "to Alaska" she seemed startled and told me that I couldn't do that. There was no choice, I had to be at work the next morning.

Through further contacts with the Center for Disease Control various things were looked into. Materials coming to me from them made it quite clear that the water had been a major problem. Among the things learned was that a connection between the plant's water and my nervous system was a probability and, given my experiences, even a near certainty. I read an accurate and detailed description of the complicated and mysterious condition, too. According to this report it might never heal. I saw that what had been experienced fit the probable contamination, across the board. A very faulted water system would turn out to be the perfect common denominator for all of it. Very professional input pointed out some possibilities for the future that I hoped would never develop, too.

Dr. Martin's report came in from Virginia Mason. It only commented about chlorinated hydrocarbons. He said that, in his opinion, our water tank would be a poor system for making those. Then he listed the possible effects of their poisoning. Those included skin problems and neurological effects, short term memory loss and difficulty in concentrating, respiratory problems, irritation, sore nose, throat or cough. A later letter said that my diarrhea was probably microbial in nature. All of this was turned over to the company. The water tank being a poor cracker was the only thing commented about or even acknowledged.

Two doctors had said that, given the nature of my exposure, there might be neurological damage. They suggested that I see a neurologist and I didn't even know what a neurologist was. I finally located a doctor, though, and made an appointment with Dr. Janice Kastella, in Anchorage.

Driving around town one day I saw that a new little strip mall was being built. I am always interested in construction and had to check that out. One of the suites had a neat sign and I asked a worker what was going to be here. He said it was to be a doctor's office. This doctor was an occupational physician. Dr. Weldon was given the list of my problems. He asked a lot of questions and told me a lot of things. I would be seeing him again. This man was thorough and he seemed to know a lot about the subject. His report, when it came in, was very detailed. A copy was sent to the company.

Any doubts that might have lingered were gone. The water was definitely to blame. The bizarre symptoms were an exact match for what could have resulted from the water system as it had existed before the clean-up. Any objective person could see it and, I believe, no objective person could miss it. One entry read that problems could include "mental aberrations up to and including seizures." Even the fact that most of my problems were intermittent turned out to fit right into what appeared to be causative and quite well documented.

Between Dr. Weldon's comments to me and his report (which did not contain some of his comments), Dr. Martin's material and the stuff from the CDC, health risks for the future were put forward. They included an "Alzheimer like condition," down the road, and various cancers. Another thing was mentioned that had not even entered my mind. This was difficulty in swallowing. There were times when it felt as if there was no hole in my throat. At the time and as all of this information was coming to me, I was not grasping the reality of what was happening. It really did seem too big to be real.

In mid-November Dr. Christian came to the job and I was called to an office at the medical department. After a little bit of talking she reached to a pile of papers on the desk. These were reports written by professionals and provided, through me, to the company. She picked one of them up and seemed to glare at me. "I do not agree with him at all," she said, "these people who set themselves up..." This lady told me that she was the only board certified occupational physician in Alaska. There was an unpleasant tone in her voice. Each of the contributors were dispatched. Apparently none of them got any respect from her.

I thought about the credentials represented in that pile of paper. They were the work of two occupational medicine doctors and a well placed PH.D. She commented about other people not being affected and I told her about George. The name was repeated and written down. Johnny had been reported to the company when I was writing to Larry Motz. That material was had by her so she should have had at least two names.

This lady told me she had worked at another place and had dealt with people who thought they had been harmed on the job. She said she told them "No contamination no problem."

I asked her why some of my symptoms cleared up when the water system was repaired.

Her answer was "the mind does funny things." Dr. Christian asked who I was going to see in Anchorage. When Dr. Kastella's name was mentioned a strong look of recognition and approval crossed this lady's face. "She'll do fine," she said.

After our meeting the doctor and I met with Allen Gillie, the industrial hygienist whose office had issued the CPS Water Quality Report. I had never met him before but remember thinking that he looked almost apologetic. We got with Bob Hartzler, Larry Motz' alternate, and went to the power plant. Everyone had an alternate. They worked when we were off duty and vice-versa. We met with Jay and all of us went back to the mechanical room.

"Show me some oil," the doctor said. I motioned to the collector pans for the bleeder system. These pans were part of the automatic system that was meant to purge the air tank and there was oil in them, as usual. Jay told her that those pans collected from the emergency generators, too.

Dr. Christian looked at the air tank and said "If you can breathe the air you can drink the water." At the time so little was known about any of this I didn't realize that no agency on earth would let anyone breathe the air in this tank. Its air had been used to pressurize water I had been drinking for more than eleven years. After the change it was still involved, but to a lesser degree, for another three.

Dr. Christian asked if anyone had seen sheen on the water. Her comment was "No sheen, no problem." Jay commented that he had never seen any. I told her about the sheen on those buckets of water and she looked as if she found that to be interesting. The lady told Gillie, who had made no comments at all, to have a sample of the air taken. I am not aware of it ever having been done.

That evening, at work, I checked the log sheets for the generators, which had not been test-run. This meant that none of the oil in those pans was from the emergency generator sets. It all came from the air tank.

My visit to Dr. Kastella was different from what I might have expected. She seemed interested and started to ask a lot of questions. It was almost like the TV psychiatrist's couch. The questions were personal; about my mother, early family life and friends. There was a follow-up visit. The doctor recommended a book called *When bad things happen to good people*. In the course of our interview she had a question for me "What do you think of your job?" I loved my job and any answer would have been an understatement. I told her how I felt and her answer, looking back, is interesting.

"Perhaps," she said, "If you like your job so much you should just forget about the water." After two visits I still did not know if I had neurological problems.

I happened to be in Anchorage one afternoon and returned to the doctor's office at about closing time. The receptionist was told that I only wanted to ask the doctor a question and didn't need an appointment. She sent me into a room to wait. The doctor came in and asked what I wanted. I asked her what the diagnosis was. "There is no diagnosis," she said. I was billed ($60, I think) for this visit. The insurance paid for most of it.

Dr. Kastella's report was received. It spoke of "a number of Somatic complaints," which meant nothing to me at the time. In my ignorance I was still in the dark. She thought some medications might help. Prozak, Tegretol and Desyrel were mentioned.

Dr. Kastella referred me to another Anchorage doctor, Paul Craig. This man interviewed me as she had. His report was inconclusive. He found that I was determined to talk about the water and had to be redirected to stay on-subject which, apparently to him, was my mental condition. His recounting of details was flawed. Just one example of this was "the patient was asked about his work schedule and he stated that he worked one week on and one week off. When he was asked why he thought seven days off would not result in a similar involvement with his diarrhea, the patient stated that there was no historical pattern to the diarrhea. This discrepancy is troubling to the examiner."

During the several years of episodes that could be as slight as ten days or as much as three weeks or more, there was no recognizable pattern. In fact, I was not keeping score and had no idea that there was anything about this that might have had anything to do with my work. With such long sieges of this abomination overlaying a week-on - week-off work schedule, who knows? The time I lost consciousness was during more than-three-weeks' duration of it. "Historically" though, at the beginning, there was a very clear cut pattern and, looking back, it was exactly related to my work. I believe that all of this was made abundantly clear to Dr. Craig.

One of his comments was particularly interesting. He said I should have been glad to have such a good job. I wondered, at the time, what that had to do with whether or not I had been poisoned. I did love my job and, coming from the very poor background I had, was in awe of where I was and of what I was doing.

Dr. Craig had a young fellow working for him. A long involved test was administered by this person. As a part of this test, questions were being asked. We went through where we were, what day it was and so forth. Then; "Who is the President of the United States?" I couldn't seem to find the right channel to direct my thought process into and struggled for an answer. This sort of thing had become, only too much, a part of my life. Finally, it came; President Reagan. I was embarrassed and commented about that to the young man. He shrugged it off and asked me who was governor of Alaska. Once again my mind was groping. A picture on the wall at the Department of Motor Vehicles kept coming to mind but no name came with it. I felt this was not the governor. That turned out to be right; it was a picture of a former one. Finally it came; Walter Hickle. I was a staunch supporter of the governor and this should have been an easy one for me. Dr. Craig's material does not mention my failures. I believe they thought I was a phony, a screwball or both.

Chapter Nine
Company Water And Company People

Dr. Christian's report finally came in and it was hard to keep from feeling sick as I read it. A lot of input was had from well placed and very competent people. I knew then, and know a lot more now, about what had happened. According to the report, she had been specifically told that no one had ever seen any sheen. She did not mention having been told that there was sheen, either. She also said no one else had been affected. My reports to her were not acknowledged and the people I cited were never approached.

Among her comments was a very interesting one. This was that if there had actually been any oil vapor in the air it would just "layer onto the surface" of the water in the tank, since there was really no way to mix the oil into solution and spread the contamination. While her idea, if true, would probably have been essentially irrelevant, Dr. Christian did not seem to have noticed an important part of the system; the two inch diameter fill-pipe located at the very top of the tall water tank. The system couldn't work if there was no water in the tank so there had to be some way to get the water into it.

About a thousand gallons of fresh cold water came into the tank through that pipe every-other-day and fell, under pressure, around ten feet, into the water remaining from the last fill-up. This was roughly like a fire-hose might be.

Thinking about it now, I see an oily and dirty air supply pushing down, at 35 pounds of pressure, onto a five foot diameter circle of drinking water. As the water is used, the air space grows in size, probably increasing both the volume and the effect of the oily vapor. The only way for water to get out of this tank is through the toilets, faucets and the drinking fountain. That water comes from the bottom of the tank, below the floating oil, which must have been fairly viscous. The contamination sediment immediately under the oil-layer was probably densest, decreasing toward the bottom but enduring to point-of-use. I would suppose that the less water there was in the tank, the closer the densest portion would have been to the discharge port, and the stronger the contamination would have been, to those points-of-use.

In short, the contamination's impact would have been at its worst before each fill-up. Perhaps in short, too; the contamination would have been very pervasive immediately after each fill-up. Along with that, edges of the descending oil-layer would have essentially "painted" the sides of this tank with oil and that oil would have gradually oozed down those sides.

I had once worked on the DEW line (Distant-Early-Warning; a line of cold-war radar sites in the arctic). At Barter Island our water came from a little lake on the tundra. In winter the increasing thickness of the ice layer drove impurities toward the bottom of this lake. As the holes needed to get to the water became deeper and deeper, the water became less and less usable. It increasingly tasted like a rubber boot smells. The water became undrinkable. It may be, and probably was, that the water system at the plant was more like that than any of us knew.

The company's water had chlorine in it. Besides contributing to the formation of chlorinated hydrocarbons it broke the oil down, sort of like a solvent might. That would have helped to integrate impurities into the solution. Light came from the sight glasses and the whole thing settled to room temperature for 48 hours; when the process was repeated. This went on for years. I can't imagine a more efficient system for mixing contaminants into the CPS water tank than what has been accurately described here, with the possible exception of a blender.

To me, the whole thing comes to a head in a serious situation.

As of March, 2008, we had six deceased cancer victims and one cancer survivor—that I know of. Including them, back then, I and one other man knew (within 2 to 3 years) the whereabouts of less than half of the people who were exposed. We knew of none of our guys having died, who didn't have cancer. The medical reports all mentioned this possibility. It was mentioned to such an extent, that I believe it should have been of glaring concern. The purpose of this book is to try to get our people who are still alive identified and monitored. Some of these men were young enough that they left families at home.

I have pled with bureaucrats for this and have submitted and re-submitted a list of names. No one has ever even acknowledged having heard about this.

As for the compressor's air entering the system after the 1987 change, this was said to be "infrequently." Having that air enter the system every-other day for about three years, in my opinion, would be significant; at the very least, enough to support long established colonies of "tough" critters. The way the bad taste episodes (an effect of those organisms) kept coming on and getting worse, after the change should be glaring proof of the fact. Besides all of this, my problems were in place well before that change, starting to show up nearly a decade previous to it.

Oil from the compressor head was said to be a "teensy bit." Lubricating oil was constantly being added to our worn out compressor. At one point, as I recall, a gallon a week.

The doctor expressed concern for my condition and offered to refer me to care givers. She hoped her explanations would be of help to me and to professionals I had seen. The report doesn't mention her telephone contacts with these people but some of them told me about the calls.

Dr. Christian said I couldn't have been harmed by something that happened "three years ago." It took a few years, after reading the report, for me to wonder about this comment. What did she know of that happened "three years ago?

Chapter Ten
What's Going On?

I had felt bad about being a bother to the company. I loved the job and was proud of B.P., too. I wore their name on my jacket and cap, had safety prizes with their logo on them, and was a strong company man. My feelings were heavy one day when I was on duty in the control area, which included Jay's office. Part of what the job was about took me in there at times.

The water quality report had cited the change to the system that had taken place in 1987. Jay's log books were on a shelf behind his desk. Places like the one where we worked record everything. This is done in bound books with their date on the binding. Seeing 1987 on one of Jay's log-books, when I was thinking about that year, a light came on. It should all be recorded. Skimming through these records sent me to the copy machine. Entries on thirteen pages presented a broad picture.

The villain was an air compressor that was overworked, worn out and pumping oil for years. An important filter was discovered to have gone for eleven of those years without an element in it. A supervisor on night shift, Walt, had changed the water system's air supply from service air to instrument air. The plant superintendent, Ben, made him change it back. Walt had then written a job request. That job request is what brought about the change to atmospheric pressure, even though the water report had presented a different scenario.

According to the log book, because of Walt's request, engineering was given a PMR; a Plant Modification Request. For any modification of company facilities to happen, management above the plant level becomes involved. A good reason for the change would be needed. At this point I still knew too little to put all of this together. Significant input would come much later from Walt, himself, who had been gone for a long time. Even after that, though, it would be some years before another information session would bring it all into focus.

An in-line oil coalescent, a device meant to drag the oil out of solution, was considered and rejected. Modifying the instrument air system so that it could handle the additional load was considered, too, but rejected because of costs. The PMR number was in the log book, along with details and the name of B.P.'s man who came to the plant on this business. John, the shift supervisor who conferred with him, had made these very detailed log book entries. Apparently Walt's original suggestion was opted for. The tank would become a reservoir with a pump and pressure tank.

Things were becoming clearer now. There is simply no way, in my opinion, that the company could not have known the truth about oil in the water. There is probably no way, either, that management could have believed the CPS Water Quality Report or Dr. Christian's report. Nothing was said to anyone about my thirteen pages.

I was working a week of night shifts and, during the day, Larry Motz was called. I didn't have a copy of the water report and wanted to study it. Larry said that he would call Gillie's office and have one sent on the computer system. When I got to the office he was busy and just said "It's there on the computer, help yourself." This copy was a little bit different than the one I had at home. There were notations, in bold type, which weren't on mine. It seemed to be more of an instrument than a report.

In summer my part of Alaska filled up with fishermen from all over the place. That's how it was when I met one of them who was the brother of an acquaintance. He turned out to be a toxicologist (expert on poisons) from the South-48. We talked about my situation. The contamination scenario was only too likely. Further, he said, the situation could be better understood if a sample was taken from the air tank.

Chapter Eleven
Company People and State People

The operation had cleared up just fine but there was a sore throat. It lasted for a long time. In the course of examination a problem was found. It had been with me all along, though I didn't know about it. This was a deviated septum. According to both the ENT man and Dr. Weldon, this could take impurities in the water and deposit them into my sinuses. All of this meant that medical people would have to go up my nose and break out something or other. When I worked for the City of Anchorage there was a man on our crew who had lived in Seward. He said there was an old doctor there who had "run an electric drill up a fella's nose, once."

I had cringed and thought "If you know about something like that keep it to yourself."

Sick leave was applied for to have the operation. Dr. Christian would not allow it. According to her, this was elective surgery and would not be covered by the company's sick leave policy.

Somewhere along the way the man from ADEC had been to the job. His visit caught me at home, off duty. When I called *The Slope*, one of the guys told me they had found oil in a pipe. Later, the man came back when I was there. He said it might have been oil. He also said that, being from a different part of the country, he was actually not familiar with these things. What I noticed most was his constantly referring to our department manager, Barney Dotson, calling him by his first name.

After quite awhile, the report came in. It was totally an *it didn't happen* thing. One comment was especially familiar and appeared to be a direct and exact quote from Dr. Christian. "Look elsewhere," it said, "for the cause of your problems." Today I marvel. A person in his position, Tim Wingerter, has been willing to accept an illegal and dangerous cross connection in a public water supply and he was able to stand behind an air compressor in a potable water system. Beyond all of this, he can go so far as to see no possible connection between these things and my symptoms.

He wrote what he wrote, though, even when health problems lined up with possible-to-probable effects of contamination in a system which never should have been allowed and was illegal but did exist, in the very place and time when the symptoms came into being. All of this was, also and significantly, when exposure and risks were possible for many other individuals. Tim Wingerter's comments to me about whether or not the system was or was not illegal simply concerned legal status, which he did not actually address in the report. A house has certain codes, he told me, and industry may not have them, at least it might not have had them, he said, back when this was done. He did not actually say if our water system had been illegal or not.

Comment was made, in the report, that these "hydro-pneumatic systems" are found in other places. I thought about the cushion tank. Those are unusual, archaic and not acceptable. They are not, however, what we had. A compressor putting its air into a public water system actually is a cross connection and is illegal. Simply put, it is violation and dangerous violation at that.

I think, now, about a friend who had lived in Anchorage during the sixties. He was a representative for an equipment company and spent a lot of time away from home, working on remote sites around the state. His wife told mine that there was something very wrong. He was having episodes of terrible diarrhea and she wondered if he had some strange sickness.

I called OSHA. The idea was that they might know about something so involved with safety. It seemed to me like I was getting the run-around and was hoping to find a way to get the air in our receiver tested. The person I spoke with said some interesting things. First was "We're not going to commit our people so that they can spend days, listening to doctors argue." I didn't know what that was supposed to mean but there was more. The OSHA man asked me if I had filed a Workers' Compensation claim. I told him I hadn't lost any time on the job. He said "That may not be the case a few years from now." The man on the phone told me that there was a form to be filled out and advised me to get it and file it with the state.

This is something that really bothered me. It seemed as if I would be trying to get something from the system. Such a thing would be against my ideas of life. Still, the situation was real. I needed to know some things and called an attorney. He too, asked if I had filled out the Workers' Compensation form. My reply was that it hadn't been done. He didn't seem to believe me. This made me wonder and I called the Workers' Compensation Division people, asking them if there was such a form. The answer was that there was and it should have been filled out when I reported the problem to the company. When the man on the phone was told that it didn't seem to have been done he said "We noticed that."

My name was on their computer, though, and I couldn't even imagine what that was about. It would be awhile before a minor incident at work was remembered. At that time a company medic had handed me a paper and suggested I sign it, saying it was a good idea.

Walt had been gone for a long time and never did get to see the changes he had requested. There was a reorganization, one of the company's constants, and he was gone. Some years later he came to my town for a hockey game and gave me a call. It would be even more years before we were to have contact again. This time it was on the phone.

In the course of talk he said "Did you know that there was oil in the water at the power plant?"

I replied that I had seen sheen on buckets out in the plant. He said he used to see it on cups of tea in the break room. This would have been handy for me to have known. I didn't comment.

Chapter Twelve
Do Something

Around seven months after my report to Larry Motz, I got off the plane and went to the office. Larry's alternate, Bob Hartzler, was there. Two things were on my mind. First, was a grievance. If someone had a beef with anything they filled out a form and the company took it from there in a formal procedure. I would never have done such a thing and didn't care much for people who did. Dr. Christian seemed to want to fight me, though, and I felt like it was time to fight back.

Bob gave me the form. "Now," I said, I want a form to report to Workers' Compensation Division."

He looked serious and said "Merv, the office in town is closed for Thanksgiving. They'll be open on Monday and I promise you'll get the form then."

Next day, I was asleep. It was mid afternoon and I was on night shift. The phone rang in my room. It was Curley, Jay's alternate. He said he needed to see me. I got up, dressed, and straightened my bed. Curley came in and sat down. He had a written communication for me from Barney Dotson, our department manager. I was being sent home, immediately. They had put me on temporary disability and I was being sent to a psychiatrist. A commercial flight would be leaving shortly.

On the way to the airport shuttle bus I stopped by the office. Hartzler was there and said "A few of us have had a sort of little meeting." Bob mentioned a management person who was known to be a friend to me, saying that he was there. "None of us know what form you are talking about," he said, "but (I allege, here) it doesn't matter because you have reported this to us, in writing." Later, I spoke with my friend, who said that Bob had asked about a form to report things to OSHA.

Boarding the plane I found myself setting next to Ben. There was a lot of pressure here. It was good to have someone I was friends with to talk to. During one of those constant changes he was put in charge of the water plant, as well as our own operation. Afterward he was removed from management altogether. Ben was an electrical engineer and found himself doing what he liked to do. It was always enjoyed, he said. We talked about the old days and then about what was happening to me. As this was going on some things began to be realized. What had been going on was not right. It looked serious, too. It was on this flight that I noticed a feeling of starting to lose respect for the company.

Once, at the camp, Larry asked me why I didn't sue the company. I told him I didn't want anything from them and those things were not my way. Too little was known at the time for me to be aware that the comp laws would not have let me sue, anyway.

The situation looked bad and my finances weren't good. Alaska had gone through a bust cycle that had hit everyone hard. People were putting their house keys on bankers' desks and driving to the South-48. Some banks had even closed. My house payment was more than sixteen hundred dollars a month. On top of that, we had two rental houses and people were not renting. Any property was a liability. Some of that was starting to clear up, though. If the job was history, maybe things could be sold.

At home, the form was obtained and filed with the state. Instructions on it said reporting was to be done promptly; in no case more than ten days after an employee reported a situation. There could be no return-ing to the job until the psychiatrist had seen me. The company made the appointment and there were commuter airline tickets to and from Anchorage for the visit. As it happened the appointment was far enough away that my surgery and recovery could take place. There would be no sick leave issue and the grievance would never be addressed.

I tried to have the company let me go to someone in my local area but they had their own ideas. The psychiatrist seemed to be a non-threatening person and his questions seemed to be straight- forward. Afterward I tried and tried, in vain, to get a copy of his report. The only thing I learned in these attempts, from people in this doctor's office, was that the company had not paid them yet.

This was during the time frame of my visit to Dr. Craig. One comment in his report was that I viewed this psychiatrist as "an agent for the company more than a competent care giver who could help (me)." The whole thing makes me a little bit sick.

It had always been my opinion that I would never, ever need a lawyer. Found now, though, was that things were looking bad. One thing had been heard over and over; "you do need a lawyer." Calling around there were referrals, which led to other referrals. Finally, an attorney was found. An older gentleman, he was quite frank. His comments were hard to believe, almost fiction-like.

"The state sold us out in 1987," he said. "Everywhere the big companies go, they push their ideas of Workers' Compensation legislation through. I worked for the state back then," he continued, "A lot of us were upset about this but we were told that if we wanted the oil industry and their money in our state these laws would have to be passed. We're not quite as bad as Louisiana but almost."

This man said that no one has any rights, where these things are concerned, outside of the state mandated program. His prediction was "they'll paint you as a nut." He spoke of some people in the legal professions and some politicians who were disturbed by these realities. According to him, companies usually harass a person until they quit. My thought was that I'd never quit and I felt like he was overdoing it. I still had a quiet respect for the company, I guess. At least that's what this attorney told my wife.

According to him the main and salient purpose for Workers' Compensation (Labor and Industries (L&I) in some states) is to make the government a part of the insurance industry. The project is to protect employers and, by extension, the insurance industry from injured workers. The method is to use government power and authority to bring this about. I had joined an unfortunate and unpopular club.

The lawyer told me my case would turn out to be especially difficult because of the potential for legal exposure. I finally realized that this is what Larry was saying when I originally reported the problem to him. Over time, others have confirmed this. One friend who is an attorney would eventually say "They have to beat you regardless of cost."

The attorney and I went to the Anchorage office of Workers' Compensation Division. We were met by a government man and an attorney for the company. I believe this was Dana Burke. He handed in a long list of reasons why he didn't think I had a case. The only one of those remembered is that I was late in reporting.

The surgery, when it came, was different from what had been done in Seattle. First, there was a form to sign. It advised me of possible risks. Blindness, brain pan leakage and even possible death were mentioned. This was not being looked forward to. However, the doctor is a sharp individual. There was a lot of confidence in him and still is. I felt that if there was a significant risk he would tell me. At the hospital I was put to sleep. The next thing was unexpected. The doctor's voice came into my mind again and again, telling me to lie very still. My heart had gone into some kind of a thing and the anesthesia had to be taken off. I was awake while they pushed their tools up my nose and pulled pieces of material out.

This heart business was new to me. Except for all of that pain in the eighties, there had never been a problem with my heart. The next thing made sense to me. A treadmill test was done and it was negative.

Chapter Thirteen
Under the Gun

Return to work was met with a letter from Barney Dotson. He said a lot of people had spent time on my "assertions." He also said I had spent a considerable amount of company time on this. That was totally false, even though this was certainly a company matter. His statement was that management had no choice but to accept the findings and documentation of professionals. He had ignored the findings of some well placed and competent people who had made a lot of input. More followed.

"What this means, exactly, is that the company will spend no more time on this issue. Accepting this position will show a great deal of professionalism on your part, to do otherwise would only be counter productive.

In today's shrinking work force, skilled employees are a tremendous asset. But to remain an asset, the employee must be willing to accept the ever increasing demands of the job and to dedicate full attention to the task at hand. To put this into perspective for your situation, you have been and are a valuable employee. Continuing your quest to find fault with the water quality… after all of the evidence shows that there has been no cause for concern will certainly jeopardize this status. Disciplinary action is not the desired outcome but when the requirements of the job can not or will not be respected, management has no choice but to invoke such action.

You, on the other hand, have a choice. Simply continue to do your job to the best of your ability, in a professional manner and leave non-job related activities to your off time."

I knew enough to be sure of what had happened. The matter was well beyond question. I also knew that very little company time had been spent on any of this. Along with all of that, I had read the reports of people who were said to have put so much time into investigating my "assertions." Those reports had problems of the worst sort. Input from professional people who were on the positive side was not even acknowledged.

In nearly sixteen years with the company and quite a few with other employers, there had never been as much as a "letter in my file" or anything like it. The person that I am would never have a cause for such a thing or put up with it. The company's credibility was fading faster than ever. I still wasn't catching on, though. It didn't even occur to me that this was a letter in my file. If Barney was production manager when the 1986 PMR was issued, he knew far more about the water system's problems than I did, going in.

The first shift back at work was one that saw something the company did from time to time. This was a review of the ethics policy. That was a well worded document, which we were required to review and, on one occasion, to sign. According to the company, they would never do anything wrong or dishonest. Specific comments were made about company doctors and industrial hygienists. They were to have especially high standards because of the professional nature of their work. Also, special consideration was to be applied where "our host governments" were concerned. We were told to report anything questionable to the Human Resources department. To me, it seemed to be a document that was designed to protect each management layer from the people below it.

It was night shift and close to midnight when Curley came to the plant, called me into the office and closed the door. He was being a little bit impatient. "You've made a lot of big guys mad at camp." He had a verbal message for me from Barney. I was not to speak of these things to anyone, except in answer to a direct question.

As Curley was leaving the plant I walked with him, still talking, through the break room and toward the door. I motioned to the coffee maker and said to look at it. He asked what he was supposed to be seeing. "The water comes through a special filter the guys put in years ago," I said, "it goes through dry coffee grounds and a paper holder. Those are probably more filters. You know that most of the water consumed around here is in the form of coffee. I don't use it." "If they would just be better about changing the filters," he replied, "when I saw them they were green."

One day Jay and I were talking. He said "If I thought, in my heart of hearts, that you had been hurt here I'd be firmly behind you. If I'm lying I'm flying." He got in two of his favorite sayings. Jay went on to say that there had been a meeting, early on, and O'Niel had put on a presentation. "He showed us drawings," he said "and they included an air compressor." (That would have been accessory equipment for a cushion tank.)

I had a comment for him, which was sort of a question. "You know that some of what is said in the water quality report is not true, don't you?" That just brought a blank look. Jay is the supervisor who got hit with this thing, twice. He tasted the water both times, recording the problem and ordering repairs. He even recorded the bad smell the second time.

One of the guys whose crew worked out of the plant came in from his time off and spoke to me. He said he had met my sister-in-law. That wasn't surprising since one of those lived in Anchorage. "No," he said, "this one is down in the South-48." It seems that he and his wife had been down there and passed through my old home area, though he hadn't known it. They met a lady there and talk had included where he worked. She mentioned me. This was quite a coincidence. There were hundreds of people on this oil field, in a lot of facilities and on different schedules. His comment, related to my wife by her sister, was "He won't be there much longer." If memory serves, this is the man who said the water tasted like oil.

One of the guys told me that he had overheard two supervisors talking about me. One of them was said to have asked the other if they couldn't just fire me. Talk around the plant was frank. My job was said to be about done. Sixteen years, in a career of around thirty, were at risk. If anything happened it would all be over. At my age a person could never replace any of this. Unknown to me at the time, too, was that someone who has had a contested Workers' Compensation claim could not find good work again if he wasn't old enough to vote, had twenty years of experience, and had three college degrees.

I was told of something that happened in the break room. The guys were talking about my situation when the man who had been inside the water tank back in 1987 spoke up. He talked about the oily waste that he had taken out of it. "That stuff came out of there by the pans full," he said. According to what I was told, Jay said this was not a good subject to be talking about. The message was received. People were not talking about this openly.

Rumors began to circulate about a RIF (reduction in force). Management was like a leaky bucket. The most intimate of details were known to everyone, at all levels, before they were supposed to be known. A mandatory meeting was called. This was about the RIF that we all knew was coming. Most of us had "secret" copies of material that had been furnished to supervisors. These things were a terror to the employees.

Years before, there had been one that was famous among us. People had gone to work in the morning. During the day busses showed up at some of the job sites. Workers were loaded up and brought back to camp. They were terminated and put on the plane to town. As we heard it, none of them were allowed to go to their rooms for personal effects or even to change clothes. Some people were stranded in Anchorage because airline tickets and credit cards were on the job. Some of the affected people were ten year employees with good work records. I overheard a man in an office who said, sarcastically, "After ten years, they won't even let a good employee go to his room to change his clothes or get his bill-fold."

We were all going to a meeting and no one was looking forward to it. A presentation was made, there, based on economics. Its upshot was that there was to be a voluntary RIF, the biggest one ever. A year's pay was offered for voluntary separation. After that, we were told, there would be two more RIFs. Neither would be voluntary and they would be less well compensated, if they were compensated at all.

After the meeting I met Barney in the hall. It had to be said and it was meant; "Barney, I'm sorry about what has happened with the water." Through clenched teeth, the manager said, "No body else got sick."

The attorney in town said "trust me you do not have a job." He had been in this field for a lot of years. He said that companies who contest a Workers' Compensation claim want to unload the guy they see as giving them trouble. They have to be very careful, though, because of the law. With a company wide restructuring going on they can do anything that they want to. "No," he said, "you do not have a job and you do not have a chance. If you need that money you'd better take it."

One of the fellows I worked with, William, said "You've always presented yourself as quite a different person than this."

I said "Different from what?"

He said "you know what I mean."

I persisted; "Different from someone who might get hurt on the job?"

"You know what I mean, you know what I mean." His voice was raising so I dropped it.

Memory comes, though. We would all be waiting in the Suburban, at camp, for the crew to gather so we could go to the plant for our shift. Someone would say "Where's Will?" The answer would be that he wasn't going to make it. It was his throat again. He liked to make a drink from the water, using a sweetened powder.

Chapter Fourteen
About Employers

When all of this first happened, I wondered about the other men. At one point I wondered if there were any others. I didn't have enough understanding, yet, to recognize the symptoms in others. I called our old family doctor. He had aged a lot; his voice was shaky and he sounded impatient.

"Everyone knows," he said, "that all people are different. Low level contamination would affect one member of those who were exposed, perhaps two or maybe even three. Mostly, though there would only be one. Perhaps some scattered symptoms might be had among the others but not too much of that, because of its low level. I asked him to write this for me and he did. A copy was forwarded to the company.

Recalled, then, was that the attorney had said it didn't matter if anyone else was hurt or not. This told me one of the reasons why. Another reason might be that some people would prefer to keep their heads down and not risk the disfavor of the company. I can understand both.

Dr. Weldon's report says he felt like the contamination was probably greater than had been thought. Looking back, now, I can only agree with this. Without that extra filter and (I believe) those coffee grounds this would have been an open book and a disaster for the guys in the office.

In my view, though, effects of this problem are far from over. Dr. Weldon, Dr. Martin and the CDC all had things to say, which may end up applying to others and to myself as well. The future might have consequences for crewmembers and, I believe, has probably already had severe consequences for some of them.

Something happened in the town of Soldotna. Their water treatment plant leaked dangerous chlorine gas to the atmosphere. There was an emergency alert and the people downwind from the plant were told to evacuate. Some people were still asleep, though, as a cloud of gas went through part of the town. One of them was an operator from the city water plant. If he had been on duty it would have been his problem. The man wasn't at work but was at home in bed. It was still a problem for him, though, but in a different way. He was taken to the hospital in a police car.

A visitor from his employer, the city, turned up. There was a paper to be signed. He was told that it was for his Workers' Compensation. Saying that he had not been on duty, he was told that since he was always on standby, he was on duty. Our man refused to sign it. We were told that it was submitted without his signature. People were wondering how he could qualify for benefits under a workers' program when he wasn't at work.

My thoughts had become a little bit different from this. To me, either something was misunderstood or there was a fly in the ointment. As already said, an injured worker has no rights in Alaska (and most other places) outside of these special interest programs. The City was looking at liability from injured people. It is my opinion that, being an employee, if this man could be put on the program liability toward him would be essentially squashed.

The city manager was a casual acquaintance. A telephone call should clear it up, at least for me. "There's talk around town that your operator wasn't on duty when the accident happened," I asked, "how can he qualify for benefits under a workers' program?" "Well," came the reply, "he wasn't on duty but there had been a prior exposure. That made him more sensitive to the gas. He does qualify, at least in a way."

A situation was heard of, which had to do with the oil rigs (drilling platforms) in the waters of Cook Inlet, off the Kenai Peninsula. These are tall metal structures standing high out of the water. They are used to pump oil from below the sea floor. Travel to and from them is mostly by helicopter. At times, though, barges are used. The men usually work a week-on, week-off, schedule. Shift change was being made. The choppers weren't flying because of weather. Homeward bound men were being lowered over the side, in a metal cargo basket, to a waiting barge. Something failed on the last load and three men were dropped, basket and all, for the last thirty feet or so.

Workers on the barge rushed to them. One fellow said "I'm okay." As the trip toward shore progressed, though, and especially as he drove toward home, he hurt more and more. A doctor's office was called, which was still several miles away, because it was near to their closing time. He would be coming in. A lady there (my wife) called his employer to verify insurance coverage. What she learned was interesting. He had been terminated. Insubordination and poor work performance had cost him his job.

I have heard that the other fellows in the basket were let go, too, but don't know what they might have done wrong.

Chapter Fifteen
The Beat Goes On

At work again, I was on night shift. My station was out in the equipment. While walking through the mechanical room, my thoughts were on Dr. Christian's visit and the oil in those pans. I saw that there was no oil in them now and thought about some of this equipment. It had been a part of my experience in several places, for a lot of years. Every one of the power plants I had worked in had a compressor and a pressurized tank. Those tanks had to be *blown down*. A valve was opened, slightly, at the bottom of the tanks and their condensation was blown out. Water was the issue and I hadn't paid a lot of attention to how oily that water always was.

The CPS air tank was bigger by far than the ones I had been used to but a compressor is a compressor and a tank is a tank. This one was huge and had accessories but it was still just another air tank. A light came on for me. Even before the bleeder system was installed in 1987, we had not been blowing it down. At its bottom was a sight glass. This was so people could tell how much water was in the air tank. There didn't seem to be any water now, though, and there was nothing in the gathering pans, either. A small valve behind the sight glass was found to be closed. Barely opening that, a column of black fluid appeared in the glass. The valve was closed as quickly as possible but not before I saw that there were many, many gallons of fluid in the air tank.

Getting a sample bottle, some of this water was obtained and examined. It was dirty, rusty, and very oily. A person can only wonder what the contamination level was of the air in that tank or how thick the floating oil layer may have been in the water tank next to it. The effect of that turbulent air against the oily water at the bottom of the air tank would have to have affected the already clouded air going to the water tank.

On day shift I told Jay there was something I wanted to show him, which had to do with the water. He suddenly turned very stern. "You've been told not to discuss this anymore," he said. Then he said I had violated a direct order. He would speak to his immediate supervisor at the department level and get back to me. I sweat bullets. It looked like my job and career were done, through a guy I had actually thought of as a friend. Friend or not, he was my supervisor and represented the company. Talking to him about the water and that order, which had been forgotten, did not seem to be related. They were.

Jay finally got back to me. He and his next in-line boss had decided to give me one more chance. I was grateful.

One day, at the camp, a man from the water department came up to me. He said that some of the guys at their plant believed me. His comment was about Henry and some discussions. This man told me to call Skip Swenson. The name sounded familiar but I didn't know who that was. He turned out to be a former employee from the alternate crew. Since we had rotated on the same day I had never met him.

I made the call and Skip said my name was familiar but that he couldn't place me. When this was all out of the way, I told him why I was calling and about the water report. Skip said that the testing results were manipulated a lot to make them come out right. His comment was "Once Jim got that filing cabinet closed what was in it became the gospel."

Further talk with him on the telephone, years later, told me something else. He said that if there is contamination involved, charcoal filters can be bad news. Skip said that they are porous enough to become strata for microscopic organisms to live in. His comment was that they can form colonies there. I wondered if this might cause the filters to be green.

The offered voluntary settlement came with a carefully worded statement, which had to be signed. It said the person really wanted the money and was leaving employment voluntarily for that reason, with nothing but the best of feelings toward the company. The attorney in Anchorage said "They're scared to death." I asked what accepting this would have to do with my Workers' Compensation case. "Nothing," he said, "that would be against the law."

A dreaded day finally came. In the camp Bob Hartzler and I sat at a small table with one of the HR secretaries. He smiled and said "are you ready to sign for the package?"

I told him the only way I would sign this thing is someone had a gun at my head literally or figuratively and the last one was the case. The secretary looked as if you could have knocked her eyes off with a stick. Bob appeared to be annoyed.

"This isn't about that water," he said.

I told him it actually was about the water and that Barney had me where he wanted me and would never let me stay on the job. Bob said he couldn't let me sign under duress. I told him that that was exactly the case.

Bob looked at the papers and then at me. "It's up to you," he said. I signed.

Back at the power plant, I was sick. Everything had gone up in smoke. Any real hope of being able to support my family was probably gone with it. All of this was because of tripping over someone else's problems. Will said it was too bad because I could have retired in just a few more years. I wouldn't have done that until I was sixty five, in 2003, but it would have been nice to have had security for those years and the chance to retire when it did come. Also, it would have been great to continue to enjoy my job.

Jay came into the break room. He asked me why I was doing this. We talked for awhile and he told me that I still didn't have to do it. He said there was a seven day period before it was effective, which is called a cooling off period. I thought "Great, but it doesn't do me any good."

The next day, as I was leaving the camp to go to work, Ben looked out of a doorway. "Hey Merv," he called, "come in here for a minute." Ben had been our plant superintendent for a long time. This was someone I liked a lot and respected the same way. In his office, we talked. He was a nice person and naturally concerned. Like it was with Jay, we knew each other fairly well.

"It's the wrong time," he was saying, "a bad move on your part. It isn't really all that much money, either."

"Tell me about it," I said, "It's a terrible thing for me."

Ben said it really didn't have to happen. He went on to say that he knew Barney Dotson. They had played golf together when he was on a trip to the South-48. Ben said Barney could be talked to and that I should go see him.

Before leaving his office, I had a question for this friend. "Since I got into trouble you've told me you always knew about the oil in our water. Is that true?" He looked a little bit strained. There was no direct answer, just a little bit of quiet rambling. "Over by the popcorn machine, a couple of months ago," I persisted. Still, there was no actual answer. Finally I just asked straight out; "Did you know about the oil in our water?" The look on his face was one nobody wants to see on a person they like.

He sort of sputtered as he said "Not in significant amounts."

At Barney's office a secretary said it would be a few minutes. I was as nervous as a cat on a tin roof. If there actually was seven days; this had been less than one day. Barney let me start to talk then he gritted his teeth again and said "trying to convince other people that they are sick, too." That wasn't even remotely true. We did talk, though, and I decided to take a chance. I really did want to be able to keep my job. I went to the office and rescinded acceptance of the separation package.

The tour of duty ended and it was time to go home. Bob said the managers had not decided what to do about my backing out of the voluntary separation. His instructions were for me to go home as if I was being separated. They would let me know if there was a change. A letter came to the house, which said the company had decided to go with "(my) original decision."

Chapter Sixteen
End Of An Era

One of the rental houses sold. There was no money in that for us but it was good to be clear of the worry. The other went on a *wrap around* sale. This meant we would still be on the hook for payments. Hopefully, the buyer would hold his end up (he didn't). Our home sold, too. It had been a dollar drain beyond belief but would be missed and losing the eventual equity was to become a huge blow for us, financially, later on. There could be no staying in Alaska. The cost of living there was just too high and there wasn't a job to be found anyway.

Larry Motz had told me I was nearly old enough to "bridge." This meant, he said, that in about six months I would be old enough to get at the deferred funds in the company benefit packages without a penalty. When some of this money finally did come through it was life saving. In fact, it is all that stood between us and total disaster. Even with the small monthly check and what I could earn, though, we struggled. It was taking away our (inadequate, at that point) retirement, too, and we were not exactly spring chickens.

Looking for work was a downer. I read the papers, made a lot of calls and went into Spokane to the employment office. There, long lines of people looked for jobs that were few and paid very little. Winter in this area is famous for being slow and summer hasn't always been a whole lot better. A year after the separation I got my first ever unemployment benefits and, probably because of the way I was raised, felt the shame of it. Bureaucrats make it clear that everyone is under the gun. The impression I got was that they want to be sure no one is getting a "free ride." When the insurance industry and human nature come together life can be miserable. Being just a number is bad enough but being even less than that can be lousy.

Our home had become a middle aged trailer house with an assumed mortgage. With no steady income, it could have been worse. A part of the reason we landed where we did was that the local school district is well known and has a good reputation. My youngest daughter was still in school. She had been "college bound" since the first grade. These things would affect that. The move was neither wanted nor enjoyed.

Looking for work was still not going well. One day there was an ad in the paper. Someone was looking for a person to drive a truck, hauling trash. It paid a small fraction of what I had been making, with no security or benefits. At their office I found what had been seen too often. There was a long line of poorly dressed guys waiting to fill out applications. While I was standing in that line a man came by and spoke. "Pardon me," he said, "are you a carpenter? We hire carpenters."

A big, single story business building had burned inside and collapsed. Everything was covered with frozen snow. Young guys were working, who drove old clunkers and looked like they hadn't been doing very well. They were a friendly, hard working bunch of kids, though. I was treated like one of their dads might have been.

One thing was conspicuous about me, that couldn't be gotten away from. I coughed, gagged and cleared my throat. "Hey man, you smoke a lot or what?" I never smoked in my life but was (and am) the one with these problems. Dr. Weldon said that my symptoms would be like those of a heavy smoker. I remember a fellow who had smoked heavily for about forty years. He was a "two pack a day" man when I knew him, and would hack and gag. Sometimes it sounded like he was yelling, in an effort to clear his throat. It was obvious and disagreeable, just like what was happening to me. It was, as so many of my symptoms were, intermittent; now I'm fine and then I'm not. Sometimes the cough in my chest could get into this. When that happened it was scary.

When payday came my wife looked at the check and said "You

worked all of that time for this?" Yep. I filed income tax and found out the company hadn't deducted from the separation money. Uncle Sam got most of what was left. The engine in my pickup went sour and took the rest.

Somewhere along the way the attorney from Anchorage wrote to me and my Workers' Compensation case began. Memories here are a little bit vague. There were formal procedures in all of this and I didn't have a clue. I found that the company's one-and-only purpose was to get me off their back. Apparently it was no big deal to the bureaucracy. The impression I came away with is that the state holds your arms while the company beats you up. I protested and complained a lot but, apparently, they had heard all of it before. Letters to just about every body did no good. Mostly, they weren't even answered. Such as did come back was just impotent bureaucratic fluff.

One of the first things told me, was to provide the company's attorneys with all medical records for the past twenty years. It seemed ridiculous if possible at all.

I did learn a few things. Supposedly, a company cannot discriminate against a person who has a claim. Harassing them or costing them their job is alleged to be, very seriously, against the law. If a company does such things, though, there are no repercussions. The state just gives the offenders "to the plaintiff in a court of law." This means that the victim comes out from under the protection of the special interest program ("Parallel legal system") and, allegedly, has rights. They become subject to powerful lawyers, fueled by apparently endless resources and power. Also a jungle of legalities, if they can afford to be involved at all and if they are amazingly fast, since there is a very tight legal "window" here.

When working class people lose, which they are virtually certain to do, the companies sue them to recover costs. A working man would probably be destroyed. A formerly working man certainly would be. Cost figures are astronomical, possibly greater than most people's net worth, and judges do not hesitate to award them to employers that are only too happy to accept them.

The company offered to settle for an amount that would have been about the size of one of my former paychecks. It was to be called a *nuisance settlement*. Given the serious nature of my situation and the possible downstream effects of that water such a thing was not going to happen, no matter what the offer might have been for. Along with this, though, and very importantly, acceptance of any money would both besmirch me and imply credibility for the company's version of these things.

The attorney wrote to me after this offer was declined. He said that if he didn't think I could win, he was not supposed to represent me. Efforts to secure other representation were fruitless. One letter from an Anchorage attorney says it all. This particular letter came before, but alludes to, some things which had not taken place yet. I think, though, that it is expressive of what I faced in trying to obtain help.

> From your letter, I am led to believe that you were an employee of British Petroleum when you were injured. You are unhappy with the way they adjusted your case and with the medical examination that they arranged. Most unfortunately, that does not distinguish you from other injured workers. I can assure you that I am no more impressed with Alaska's comp system than you are. There does, however, seem to be very little that can be done about it. While our supreme court has given lip service to the concept of potential bad-faith claims against employers and their insurance carriers in the Workers' Compensation context, that is about all that it has amounted to, to date. The Alaska Supreme Court has refused to affirm any punitive damage recovery in the insurance bad-faith setting for many years.
>
> While I am not willing to tell you that you have no claim or that your claims are impossible, I am willing to say that I am unable and unwilling, as a business matter, to undertake your case. I can do nothing to preserve your rights…

I was suffering with some of my symptoms and inquired about help. No one felt like they could do the testing needed to find out what was wrong inside. I heard of a group in Seattle who could probably handle it. This was Harbor View medical center. I wrote to them but they didn't get back to me. I made another try at that but they still didn't answer. When I called there, someone said no one was available to speak with me. Finally, one evening, the phone rang in my home. It was Harbor View. A lady was finally returning my call.

"You can prove nothing," she was saying.

I told her that my problems were more important to me than "proving" anything. This went on. Finally, I asked if someone could write and offer me some suggestions.

Among other things, she said "Nothing in writing."

I asked if she was saying what I thought she was saying. A quiet answer let me know all she wanted for me to know. For some reason, I wasn't welcome at their place of business. They wanted nothing to do with me.

Chapter Seventeen
Life After B.P.

I had submitted copies of the log sheets and an overview of them to the Workers' Compensation Division. Also furnished, was a copy of the CPS Water Quality report, with its overview. Everything had to be shared with me and material received showed that BP's lawyers protested introduction of the report as evidence on my side. I still had no idea how any of this worked. It seemed to me that the protest was accompanied by an attempt to deceive. The document was identified as anything but what it was. My letter to the board, describing the alleged deception, was not answered. I was left to wonder if no one cared or if there was some point being missed because of my ignorance.

I was amazingly ignorant but suppose that some of these people would be confused, too, if they were called on to build a house or to parallel generators. In answer to questions asked, I was told "We cannot give you legal advice."

The company said I had made off with unauthorized copies of log book entries. That was true and I felt no need to apologize. They also said I had raided the computers before leaving. Computers baffle me and could not have even found my way into them, let alone "raid" them. My old word processor gave up the ghost a few years ago. There are no more to be had or to be repaired. It's a computer or a ball point pen, for me. I'm typing this on a three hundred dollar lap top and it's driving me nuts. A friend set up the files for me and I lost my material, over and over again. My daughter finally saw my predicament and installed a better program, made new files and set up icons on the screen so that I could get into them. A grand-daughter saw something I was doing wrong and offered a very helpful suggestion. I can't do any of the moving words around thing or anything else computers are so famous for – this book might be a lot better organized if I could. A friend has to send this to the publisher because I wouldn't have a clue about how to do that. Hopefully all of this will gradually change but, so far, it doesn't look good.

Back in the spring of '93, one of my sons told me about the construction boom in Wal-Mart country. I made a trip to see if there was something there that might lead toward some form of financial security for my family. This put me in touch with Charlie, Clyde and some other people who were working their tails off and barely making it.

The subdivisions where we worked saw a lot of buyer activity after work hours. Usually the framing crews were still there. For some of us the jobs didn't pay by the hour and for all of us there was no pay until a project was far enough along for the builder to get a draw from the bank. One evening we were on a roof. Clyde looked down at the realtors and their prospective clients. "Any of them can become what I am," he said, "but not all of them can become what I was." None of the guys on these crews could qualify to buy a house.

I had problems and was still thinking there were real medical people out there somewhere. Surely, testing could be done and a way found to help me. The problem was that I had no idea who or what to look for. I went into a doctor's office and asked a lady at the desk. She told me they were not allowed to give out information. Only a doctor could do that and it would require an appointment. A small clinic came to mind, then, where I had seen a sign saying they didn't make appointments. Their fee was a flat thirty dollars for an office call. I decided this might be my chance to find out what kind of doctor I was looking for.

The receptionist took my money and showed me into an exam room, handing me one of those gowns that leaves your naked back end shining out. I told the lady that I only wanted to ask the doctor a question and didn't need the gown. She said the doctor wouldn't see me if I wasn't undressed and in that gown.

Standing in the room, naked except for a drafty piece of cloth, I came across a copy of the Readers' Digest, which had an article about a plane crash near my old air base in Greenland. That was being read when a young doctor came in and asked what I wanted. I looked up from my magazine and said I needed to know what kind of a doctor to go to, in order to find out what was wrong with me.

My situation was explained. The doctor said that he would probably look at that a little bit jaundiced. He did tell me who to see, though, and an appointment was made. Those people were nice. The doctor and his office manager called me into a room and said they really could not become involved. There was no charge.

A lot of people who were working on those houses in '93 were working *under the table*. This is to say that they weren't licensed and did no formal book keeping. I told Charlie that these guys thought they were contractors just because they could frame a house. I also said that if anyone ever did a head-stand out of the rafters onto a concrete slab the state would come in here and clean house. I took a license and bid to a company doing insurance restoration work.

One job I got from them was rebuilding a house that had been firebombed. Its owner was a doctor. I asked the man I was bidding to if the doctor was an abortionist. He wasn't and I wondered what this fellow had done that had made someone so mad at him. It was on this job that the second awful pain, which had hurt so much, came back. It came on, as it always did, in my sleep. During the first few years after the water was cleared up it came back from time to time. Episodes usually lasted for a few weeks to a month or so. There could be no working. I headed for Spokane, in pain and mostly driving with one arm. Too bad; what I was doing in Arkansas looked as if it might have worked into something.

Chapter Eighteen
Facing The Real World

Medical reports had been coming in. Whatever was received by the opposing lawyers had to be shared with me. Dr. Bender's report to them was interesting. This is the doctor I had gone to after the episode on the Alaska Highway. He is the one who decided to send me to the specialist in Anchorage. Though neither of them was able to determine the cause of the clear water problem, the new man seems to have been more on his toes. His report says "He (meaning me) denies the drinking of water from wells or from streams." Apparently, this fellow knew what could have caused my problem. However, at the time, no one knew about what was happening at work, including myself.

His report, which was addressed to Dr. Bender, said that he was unsure of the problem's cause but suspected "psychological problems, as (they had) discussed." These ideas had originated with Bender. Apparently he had his own thoughts about what could be causing the problem. In fairness, he didn't know about the water, either, but there turned out to be things about him I wasn't aware of.

This man's report commented about my religious preference by name (misspelled) and called me a *moralist*. Some years later these things were mentioned to a friend. He said that he couldn't believe I had gone to Dr. Bender. As it turns out, there was mutual acquaintance here and, because of this, the doctor knew who I was, apart from any professional situation. Bender is affiliated with a religious group that is openly critical of other people's beliefs, apparently including mine.

Both doctors got details wrong. Bender would be quoted freely, though, as the Workers' Compensation process continued. His grasp of what was told to him was the poorest of the two and, I think, even poorer than most of the medical people involved, which wasn't particularly great. Along with that, he appears to have invented whatever pleased him. Cleaning up the water where I worked did wonders for my *psychological* problems. That diarrhea has never offered to come back.

I would find Dr. Kastella's report to be well used, too. A few years were to go by before I understood what the word somatic means. This term is reserved for people who have internal emotional problems. They are not aware of them. These things hurt so much, though, that the pressure manifests itself in physical symptoms. Some things in the reports, though problematic and even false, began to be understood.

My request for reports from Virginia Mason was never answered but I got them through the sharing process. Remembering my arrival at the Virginia Mason Clinic and that encounter with Dr. Yarrington; I believe what he did to me, a supposedly total stranger, was bizarre. I also believe Dr. Christian had called him and that he realized who it was that had just come in from Alaska. Most of what he described to me about this new thing did not apply to me. A taste in my mouth like pepper? Nope. A taste like vomit? Nope. Sore throat? Oh yes— and heartburn, too. Belching? No. That tube being pushed up my nose makes sense to me, now. It was a search for reflux. I know, now, too, what it meant when a lady told me the valve was working. This was not reflux, which was heard of for the first time, that morning, at Virginia Mason Clinic.

Even though Dr. Yarrington did not see me, he filed a report and I find that to be interesting. It says "There is no correlation to be obtained" between my symptoms and the water which, technically, he should not have known about. I was at the clinic five days, though, involved with other members of their staff, dealing with things besides the lesion. He didn't seem to be aware of that.

He says "(I) was seen today with a history of gastro-esophageal reflux."

My thought was *seen*, by whom? Also about whose history this might be and where it was found. It was all news to me and probably would have been to any doctor I had ever seen, as well.

The next Virginia Mason report was from a doctor who did a very specific test. Dr. Gelfand's comments show a lack of information about details of my case. He actually had no information to go on other than the fact that there was a lesion on my vocal chords. Along with this, what he did could not have told him anything beyond the very small matter he was involved with.

In spite of this, he wrote "rule out environmental cause," which about blew me away. I simply cannot find a connection between what he did and what he said. He wrote that a test would be done to try to rule out reflux. According to his later report the test was a "borderline study." Information given me pointed out how this contamination could damage my esophagus. If there had actually been such a problem it could have just been another result of the water department's mess-up, anyway.

Other people who were seen at the clinic had different ideas.

Some years later, in reply to a written inquiry from me, one of them called my house. He had gone into his records and re-read my case. This doctor said what he saw back then could have been caused by the contamination I described but that I would never be able to prove it. Nothing was offered in writing.

Chapter Nineteen
We All Die, Merv

I could be awfully sick when some of my symptoms were at their worst. I once told a man from our HR department that I felt like I might die when I was so sick. He said "We all die, Merv." During one of these bouts of sickness a doctor was seen. He both said and wrote that water contamination, as described to him, could have caused what he was seeing. His report would eventually be held out of evidence by the company's lawyer. A second doctor, referred by this first one, did a tread mill test. That test was stopped when a problem showed up. Apparently the situation that had stopped my septum surgery was still with me. CDC material had touched on my heart. I didn't feel anything but suppose whatever had happened was still around. (2007) It appears to be gone now but I still have an irregular heart-beat, which was heard of for the first time when Dr. Bender examined me after the incident on the Alaska Highway.

Once, when the sickness was bad enough, I went to my doctor. He felt that I needed to see someone more specialized and an appointment was made. When it was time to be seen, though, I was better and there were no symptoms. This doctor, just being told what the sickness was like, commented about reflux. I did not have it, never have had it, and told him so. The fellow was determined, though, and showed me pictures of people's burned out throats. He ordered an elaborate and expensive test for reflux. Results, he said, were that the valve was "leaking slightly."

A few years before that, another determined doctor at Virginia Mason had said it was a "borderline study," which seems to be saying the same thing. Neither had found what they were looking for. Neither had seen or heard anything to lead them to this, either. This new doctor gave me some medication and told me to sleep with my head up. I did take the medication but never bothered to do the other. It was too uncomfortable and wasn't needed anyway. I do not, and never have had, reflux.

Billing for this doctor's test was declined by Workers' Compensation Division and the cost went onto my medical insurance. Even with their part paid, what came back to us was a burden. Given our dismal financial picture, even with the company provided insurance, I needed to avoid doctors. We went back to making payments. These bouts of awful sickness moderated and went away. It's been a long time since I have had one.

Workers' Compensation Division procedures were taking place. Every so often I got a letter. Those letters notified me of another telephonic pre-hearing conference. This was supposedly so we could frame issues, resolve conflicts, and so forth. It was all based on the alleged good faith of the company and its attorneys. There were some issues, no doubt about it, and the government was not willing to hear about any of them. Just one of those was the amount of time the company had gone without reporting. They explained that the elapsed time of more than seven months was spent "sincerely investigating." Only after determining that there "might" have been a problem (and after I had reported it) did they report a situation which was to have been reported "in no case" in more than ten days.

A contractor friend who had a dozen or so employees said "You only have about ten days to report these things or you are in deep trouble with the state."

As for my allegations that Motz had told me I had done all I needed to do, they noted that he was no longer with the company and would have to be located. Thrown back at me again was my being late in reporting.

It may be that the company's investigation took about twenty minutes and might have been done in the industrial hygienist's office or even just on the phone; the problem must have been obvious to the hygienist. The company's (I believe) ostensible investigation took about three days, resulting in a very troubled report. Months later, Dr. Christian finished things up and wrote her report, which is no better.

Both documents were dated before the matter was reported to the state, and that date had become the formal "date of injury." I wanted for these things to be a part of the evidence. My idea was that lying and manipulating, such as I seemed to be seeing, showed company knowledge of the affair and of its potential for harming people. An attempt was made to get the date of injury changed to reflect the actual time of my report to Larry Motz, which was documented. That bounced, even in writing.

During one of the telephonic pre-hearing conferences I mentioned going to the doctor.

The company's new lawyer, Mr. Wagg, commented, "That wasn't for medical reasons, was it? Weren't you just building on your case?"

During one of those conferences I mentioned the breaking of the state's laws.

Their man, Mr. Grossi, said "You wouldn't want for some one to go to prison, would you?"

This seems to tell me that what I was alleging was actually illegal. It also seems to say that the state's people were aware of my allegations and that those were correct. In the case of the reporting issue, alone, they had absolute knowledge. I had the distinct impression that all of this was against me.

This is being rewritten after another one of our guys, Fred, has died. If the state had taken my first request seriously, when it was made (we had already had some cancer victims), four people that I know of, who are now dead, might have been saved.

Chapter Twenty
Get Help

On two occasions Mr. Grossi told me that if things were as I thought them to be the attorney general's office should be contacted. After the second of those recommendations I decided to have my try. My letter to them said I knew they had nothing to do with it if the company discriminated against someone (though it is said to be illegal.) This was not about that.

The problem, I believe and alleged, was that the company was defrauding the state. In her answer, Kristin Bomenegan informed me that her office has certain functions. Apparently what was described did not fit into their operations. "Buck passed," I thought. An attorney general's office that doesn't get involved if the state is defrauded? My answer went right back. They did not appear to understand what I was saying. Then it was Ms. Bomenegan's turn and she did not know what I wanted. This sort of thing went on for a while. Finally my letter was very short and to the point. Parts of it were in **bold type** and some of it was underlined. The letter writing had been an orderly and non-productive back and forth but now there was just silence. A few months went by. Finally, a short letter was written to this lady. She was told I was not a dog, a fool, or a miscreant and that I demanded an answer.

From the Attorney General's office of the State of Alaska, came a large brown envelope. In it, were all of my letters, each in its opened envelope. A short note said that mine was "a dispute with (my) employer (and) nothing more." Their files were clean.

O.S.H.A. had not been willing to have any interest. Now the attorney general's office didn't want to be involved, either.

Overviews of the C.P.S. Water Quality Report, Dr. Christian's report and the Shift Supervisor's log book entries were done so a layman could understand what was being seen in each of them. Any interested person, who was willing, could see right through it. Nobody commented or even acknowledged hearing about them.

Chapter Twenty-One
It Goes On And On

A lawyer was coming to Spokane, from Anchorage. Mr. Hutchins represented the company. I was to be officially videotaped in some sort of a legal thing. He laid a paper in front of me. It was a copy of one of the log book pages, on which the words *in line oil coalescent* were circled. Mr. Hutchins asked what this meant. What it meant, of course, was that our drinking water had been fouled with lube oil to a point where the company had considered using a mechanical device to try to draw the oil out of solution.

In the interview he asked what kind of poisoning I was alleging. I mentioned hydrocarbons. He asked what I knew about such things. Then he hit me with "Everything is made out of carbon; this table is made out of carbon."

It strikes me as singular, perhaps; strange at best, that I could be under-the-gun so badly because of a drinking water system where a mechanical device for drawing oil out of solution could even be thought of; no matter what might be made out of carbon.

I had written to the company's VP in Anchorage, telling him what was thought of these things and how the ethics policy was being mocked. That brought a letter from the lawyer who represented the company at that time, saying any correspondence was to go through him. I wrote to the company's CEO in London. He replied that he was confident that his "colleagues at exploration" had done nothing wrong and advised me to pursue my Workers' Compensation case.

During this taping the attorney said "Suppose that the company doctor was as you say; corrupt, out to get you and all of the rest, what about other doctors and professionals?"

The answer, of course, if I'd have been on my toes or could have had a lawyer who was, should have been a question for him. What about all of the material in your files that is clearly in my favor? It's from doctors and professionals too. Why won't anyone even acknowledge that it exists?

He commented that I had excellent insurance, which I see as being not only totally irrelevant, but inaccurate. Mine was not that. It came through the company.

After the taping was complete I had a suggestion for this lawyer and for the company. The whole situation might be corrected without a lot of problems for anyone. Reinstate me. It would bring the job back that had meant so much and getting some medical help would be possible again, too. This could right the wrong in so many ways. Word came back that the company didn't see it as an option.

Once I happened to read Dr. Weldon's report to the state. It seems to fit here. "… recommend … continue to work with B.P. to investigate the source of possible exposure to contaminants and work out an equitable arrangement to deal with (my) medical problems."

One letter from W.C. had a new name on it. A woman's, it was labeled "Workers' Compensation Specialist." Comments made by this person during telephonic pre-hearings as well as one in writing, made me feel that Ms. Gaal was more against me, than she might have been objective.

One of those telephonic pre-hearings was scheduled. This was when I was in Arkansas and neither had a phone or was working where there was one. This meant a drive into town, with a certain telephone booth in mind. Then I became aware that I was way out on the other side of town, just driving along. Information from both Dr. Weldon and the CDC was that cognitive problems would probably endure, perhaps even worsen. Finding myself out there like that scared me. When the call was made I told the people what had happened. Someone on the other end of this conference call laughed.

An offer came from the company. It was for about six weeks, gross pay. This was said to be because they did not wish to spend more money in addressing my case. Some of what has been going on with me may never heal. Dr. Weldon didn't think much could be done for a lot of it and said so. Also, there were future risks laid out; both in the report and in his personal comments to me. Among them, that "Alzheimer-like condition" seems to be of special concern, along with various cancers set forth in the CDC material. Still, there is hope.

If help is ever available it ought to be within reach, especially if things get worse. It can never happen, though, as long as the causative is denied and my situation is tied to a defeated (or settled) Workers' Compensation case. Things probably cannot be accurately diagnosed, either, if the causative is denied. That denial would an effect of the settlement.

There is more. It includes getting the run-around like I allege happened, losing my job and career and all of the downstream misery for both my family and myself. The list continues with people's being able to do things that seem to be so basically wrong and to ram it all down my throat. The *clean file* syndrome is strong and in keeping with legal terminology. (*Injury did not arise out of or in the course of employment.*) Striking out in any direction (*The mind does funny things.*) Directly, I allege, lying and/or rationalizing (*To decrease, by one, the number of pressure vessels.*) It goes on and on.

Along with that, the amount of money offered would not have had any real effect on my financial situation, which was a direct result of all of what had happened. Also, it was as it had been before; accepting their offer would have been implication that their version of these things was correct. Second, would have been tacit confirmation of the idea that I was after their money. In very real fact, I never was after their money and never did ask for any of it. At one point down the road the company would tell the Workers' Compensation Division they had tried to settle.

Apparently, to some folks, these were a bunch of nice guys who had been set upon by a money monger. The lawyers had written that they were in their "defensive mode."

A part of my reply said their money should either be held by themselves or their insurers to be applied to the cost portions of possible medical care and that I should be reinstated. Refusal of the offer brought a letter from Mr. Hutchins. My reply to it probably wasn't flattering to him. Another letter came to me, then. He said that if I thought a better offer would be coming, it wasn't going to happen. To me, this was both revolting and insulting.

In the process of legally mandated sharing I had finally gotten a copy of the psychiatrist's report. It saw me as being clean, where mental problems were concerned. It said that I did not want anything from B.P., but felt they should acknowledge that there was something wrong with the water system. None of this has ever changed.

Also a part of this sharing, were some more of the medic's notes. I learned that *supervision* was alleged to have been behind getting me to a psychiatrist. It was said to be because of my *unusual and disruptive behavior … last week.* That would have been when I filed a grievance against Dr. Christian's opposition to my surgery and requested a form to file a Workers' Compensation claim with.

That entry says *for the record* and is signed by Dr. Christian. The entry just above it is also her work. It says the psychiatrist said there was no psychiatric condition, so there was no reason to waive discipline if I became disruptive. That, in my opinion, translates to firing me if I continue to allege on the job injury. Remembered here, is that the situation had not been reported to the state as this was written.

I was actually surprised at the volume of material from the medics. These people referred to me as a "difficult Historian." That's probably professional jargon for a hypochondriac. It's a little bit embarrassing until I reflect on what the symptoms were and about how hard that water hit me at times. Embarrassment fades, too, when realization is had. I was looking for something, once and got out an old briefcase. Inside, was a part of a roll of those powerful throat lozenges, a partial tube of hydrocortisone cream and some Tums. It was like a blast from the past. As badly as they were all needed at one time, none of them are needed anymore.

It reminds me of one of our guys, Slim, who quit the company in '86 and went to work nearer to his home. I talked to him some years later, by phone, in setting up the Workers' Compensation hearing. He told me that when he had worked with us he had skin problems on his hands. He said that some of the old ointments and creams he had used back then were still around his house. The problems went away after he left the *Slope* and, I believe, got away from the water. Mostly, he was on the other crew so I didn't see his rash, if that's what he had.

The last report from B.P.'s medics was interesting. I had just come in from Virginia Mason. It was about eighteen hours after my surgery and I thought it would be a good idea to check in with our medics because of that. He was told about my believing the water at work had harmed me. His written comment was *Difficult Historian*.

Chapter Twenty-Two
Closing Ranks

The company's people were working toward getting me to an Employer's Medical Evaluation (EME). Ostensibly, this is about their right to have the patient examined by someone of their choosing. An appointment was made for this, in Seattle. It was with a group who called themselves Medical Consultants Northwest. Plane tickets and lodging were provided.

There were problems here, where I was concerned. Reading through medical reports, it happened again and again. My own situations are familiar to me. Also known, is what doctors have been told. Reading their reports has often been revealing. They can be confused, sometimes way off base, even contradicting what has been told to them. At times it appears that the doctors have invented what ever suits them. It would be impossible to reconstruct my situation using these reports. Some things are reported that are simply false and, at times, even impossible.

The solution seemed simple enough. A small tape recorder would preserve what I had told these people. Setting in the waiting room, a lady brought a message to me from the company's attorney in Anchorage, Mr. Burke. I was to go into the EME without my tape recorder. That was refused.

While I was waiting, the receptionist was overheard answering her phone. "Oh, no," she was saying, "We only work for corporations and government agencies." After awhile, the office manager came to me with another message from Anchorage. I was directed to go into the EME without my recorder. The attorneys said that they had no objection, themselves but if any one of the doctors had a problem with it, there could be no recorder. I refused again.

Among the ladies who were working in the reception area I overheard that one of the doctors had said he was objective. Finally, though, I heard that one of them would not allow my recorder.

"You are free to leave," the office manager said.

My comment was that I came here for the EME.

"Nevertheless," she said, "you are free to leave; you may go home."

I still have her voice on tape.

My wife said I had made them mad. She had suffered a lot, for a long time. Now there was fear. Her concern was about what might happen if they went after me. To lose a nice home, two rental houses and a good job and career at fifty-five is bad enough but to just have an equity in an old trailer to lose and possibly a judgment on top of that might actually be worse.

One of my brothers-in-law was a retired executive from a huge corporation. He said "You're lucky to be alive. These people take things like this seriously."

My wife felt like they were probably capable of about anything and powerful enough to get away with it. She also felt that the government is behind big people and their money. To my mind, that is an obvious fact. In hers, it would be better to just take what was offered, swallow hard, and get into line with the never ending string of victims; too often, then, to be seen as a deadbeat or a money monger. It seems to me that the word frivolous is often used frivolously.

A doctor friend was asked if that tape recorder should have been a problem. He said "Not unless you have something to hide." Workers' Compensation Division was petitioned by the company's attorneys. There was an opportunity for me to reply and that was done. The board decided to let it pass. However, I was told, there would be another EME. I was instructed to go to it without a recorder.

The big day finally arrived. The EME was in the Cabrini Medical Tower, overlooking Seattle. Three people sat on folding chairs, there, against a wall. I was on another one of those, looking back at them. These were doctors. Memory seems to say there was a fourth person involved in their work. The two who come to mind just now are Dr. Michael Allison, the lone male on this panel, and Dr. Brooke Thorner, their psychiatrist. A third person's name was Von Preyus but I don't recall anything about her except for being of a light complexion and appearing to be young. Other people seemed to be involved but reports were not always clear to me.

There were times when my voice sort of went strange and made me talk funny. My wife said that, when this happened, I should just stop talking. I called it my Teflon voice. The throat doesn't get hold of words, sometimes. It seems to be a part of the stuff that I've lived with over these chemicals. Dr. Thorner looked up and said "What am I hearing?" Her report would say it was a little bit like a yawn. It became less and less of a problem and I haven't noticed it lately.

We talked and a lot of questions were asked. Afterward there were separate interviews. One of those was with Dr. Allison. He seemed to be vaguely familiar and did the physical, which was a very limited thing and probably couldn't have told him much of anything that mattered. I suppose that the examination is probably just a part of some legal apparatus, which says that he did examine me.

In conversation with, him Dr. Martin's name was mentioned. He said "Did you see Dr. Martin? I didn't notice his report." Examination of materials was an important part of this group's assertions. Still, Dr. Allison seems to have missed one of the very key documents. At one point he mentioned Dr. Weldon's material, saying he admired it. Another thing in Dr. Allison's remarks was interesting. Concerning our water system, he said "There must be hundreds of them."

My thought, now, is *name two*.

Dr. Allison asked if anyone else had been affected. Those people had been mentioned in what I had furnished to the EME. He said, "I mean besides those." I started to talk about things that had been seen among the crew members. While he had appeared to be rather lethargic before this, Allison came to life here.

He shut me off quickly. "You're the only one with a Workers' Compensation claim, aren't you?"

My reply was in the affirmative. I was the only person on the crew naive enough to do that. (Since the guys have been dying of cancer, though, I'd do it again; in a heart-beat.)

After this there was an interview with Dr. Thorner and a written test similar to what had been done in Dr. Craig's office. In not too long a time the EME report, which was totally against me, came to the house. Its contents were, besides being amazingly one sided, sometimes amusing. Comment about my not drinking coffee was that I didn't drink coffee "at the time." This would be my life "time," I suppose. If you are a kid who has never tasted coffee and who washes the dishes, trust me, the smell of a coffee pot can make sure you will never drink the stuff. Another comment was that I had fainted after eating a piece of candy. Something was found to allegedly account for, or at least to shade, apparently, each item.

Some things appeared to be cut out of whole cloth. Some were, too and in my opinion; strikingly obvious and rather clumsy direct lies. Those seemed to be significant and directly on-subject.

According to the report, I was beset by a wide variety of things. None of them had anything to do with drinking water. Psychological problems appeared to be rampant. Somatic (I finally learned what that meant) and schizophrenic, I was in bad shape. Around ten years ago a man took a rifle into a public place. He killed some people and wounded others. Shot by a police SWAT team, he turned out to be a diagnosed Schizophrenic. When this was heard about, memory came to life and, with it, some indignation. *Have I become a diagnosed Schizophrenic?*

My aunt had known me since I was a toddler. A former professor, she was retired from the psychiatry department of a major university. I told her about the schizophrenic thing and she said I was not schizophrenic. Then she looked right at me for a moment and said "… no …" very quietly and rather thoughtfully. It was the first time I had even thought of my aunt in her professional role and I believe that I had just been examined far more and much better than I was at Dr. Thorner's office.

Symptoms that had gone away fit right in. Somatism was satisfied because I was able to *fixate* on the water system. I had something to blame things on; a sort of a pressure relief valve, I guess. One comment said I was totally out of touch with my feelings, wanting to be seen by others as being composed, virtuous, (etc.). Actually, I am squarely in my comfort zone. The man is, very much, what the child was.

Dr. Thorner's report said that I was "self effacing." I doubt if this is true at all, especially in the way that she seemed to mean it.

In 1999 I saw a special on TV about a suspected link between psychology and cancer (which, in my opinion, besides possible liability, may be the big concern here). It seems, according to this program, that a lot of folks who develop cancer are seen as being self effacing and so forth. Dr. Thorner's diagnosis of me was closely echoed here. My mother once told me that there had never been a cancer victim in any of my blood lines. I've got heredity going for me. There is also a clean lifestyle. I finally realized, too, that passing all of that clear liquid probably got a lot of the bad stuff out of my system.

I had thought that drinking the water might have been my downfall because the other guys had better (filtered) water, in the coffee they drank. As it seems to be working out, though, the light stuff, which is what gave me all of that trouble, seems to have been all they avoided; to the extent that they may have avoided it. The really bad stuff (long-chain hydrocarbons?) was still in their coffee. Hopefully, I got rid of that with those years of profound clear water diarrhea. I believe the cancer epidemic among our people is related directly to what was capable of making it through the filter and those coffee grounds.

Along with everything else, I was "hiding something." A person who uses my "rigid self control" to conceal "hostile urges," I avoid other people. The doctor might excuse my inclination to smile. Our facility was well known and was often visited by groups of touring business guests. Most of the fellows would rather hide than to take a group of them through the plant. On our crew, those tours often fell to me. They were enjoyable. I met folks and showed off stuff that actually meant something to me.

Most of the guys, too, would rather have had a root canal than to serve on the company's committees. For our facility and on our crew, that was for me. Once, at camp, a second line supervisor came toward me, shuffling a stack of envelopes. One of those turned out to be mine. It was an appreciation bonus for serving on committees.

The check inside was for five hundred dollars. No one has ever accused the company of being tight.

At this time I serve as a volunteer at a prison. I was invited to do this and accepting the call has turned out to be a good thing. I do not avoid other people and never have.

The members of our school board might have disagreed with Dr. Thorner's assessment, too. One matter, especially, was such that it became a divisive issue. The situation found me in the thick of it as a member of the parents' advisory council to the school board.

As for hostile urges; my whole life has been spent as the gentle guy. I don't know if I'd actually know how to hit someone but have never had the urge or the need to do it, in spite of some of Dr. Thorner's ideas. I'm pretty much soft hearted and my wife says that I cry at card tricks. One of my daughters was told about the hostile urges comment. She had majored in psychology. Her reaction was a big smile and a comment. "Boy," she said, "she sure got a wrong number. You're the least hostile person I know."

I don't hunt because of not wanting to hurt animals or caring for blood and guts. Growing up at a time and place where all boys took their first deer at twelve or so, I have never killed one and do not want to. More than twenty-six years in Alaska saw no hunting. At work, Slim said that it was unnatural. If there are hostile urges, I'm not aware of them.

"He is quite uncomfortable in situations calling for anger or conflict." In a lot of ways that is and always has been, true. I'm very put off by anger or bluster. To me, it's unbecoming and very distasteful. This is probably because of both how I was raised and my own native temperament.

Noted in Dr. Thorner's report was that there were "no stressors." Apparently, to her, nothing would account for there being any particular stress in my life. Reflecting on her comment brought memories. Years of chronic clear water diarrhea, a foul stinging rash on my knuckles, two kinds of terrible pain, awful chest pains and heart burn, hacking, coughing, choking; A hard to describe condition that went on and on and still does today. There were and are apparent cognitive problems, two unwanted operations and weird things happening with my heart, losing consciousness behind the wheel, nearly killing my kids. Also, there is professional input about possible problems for the future.

The list continues with the fight that erupted at work with the report of my long-lived diarrhea and its having vanished as our water system was cleaned up for the third time and actually repaired for the first time. There might be a little bit of stress in experiencing hypocrisy, threats, lies and intimidation, too, as well as loss of job and career. A big part of my life was going down the tubes and harm was being done to my retirement, as a near-to-senior citizen.

Situations surrounding low end jobs and chronic unemployment as an older man might have caused some worry, too. The family was devastated and, in many ways, much of our life was blasted. An unwanted move to an unwanted situation and the helpless of not being able to fight any of it didn't feel great, either. A blind-sided system that was mindlessly doing their thing, while I was being battered, made me feel things I didn't do well with, at times, too. A mailbox that was constantly producing letters from a "legal office" in Anchorage and official stuff from the bureaucracy were just icing on the cake. Stress? Probably, but none of was causative to anything—it was all caused; but I think I took it fairly well.

I can add to all of this, what Dr. Weldon said about how this contamination could cause seemingly emotional things and that the situation might generate stress. He recommended counseling on an "as needed" basis for it. His comments were written before the company and those who followed in their wake tore into me, too.

Dr. Thorner said there might be at least some stress because I was "starting a business." At my age, after returning from Arkansas, finding a realistic job seemed to be out of the question. My best experience was in a field that was essentially shut off to me. The second line of hope was carpentry, a trade where opportunity is naturally limited, even for guys who are of a productive age. The only way I could have anything at all was to get a license and struggle for work. In Washington State, you can't work without a license, unless you are employed by someone else who has one. The EME team became aware of the license during our initial interview and apparently, in Dr. Thorner's mind, this was "starting a business."

Dr. Thorner said I was worried about my health. Dr. Bender had reported critically about my attitude. He said I had no interest in my health. Actually, it's somewhere between the two; more toward the not overly concerned part, especially when it comes to formal exercise, which is what we were talking about. Some of the guys on the crew had a groupie thing going in the gym after work. In their mind, if a person wasn't all fired up about pumping iron they were going to die tomorrow and it served them right. I don't drink or smoke, eat very little meat, use no substances, sleep well, work hard and am not a pill popper. I used to kid Jay, who is younger than I am and one of the groupies, saying I'd come to see him when he was in the old folks' home.

Dr. Thorner pointed to a lot of psychological things. Dr. Christian, quoting a psychiatrist, said there were no mental conditions, so I could be (fired).

In passing and still on Dr. Thorner; she mentioned "malingering." I found this comment to be offensive. I worked in a saw mill at fourteen, on a wheat ranch at fifteen and (being upwardly mobile, I suppose) on a railroad section gang at sixteen. In rural America, during the fifties, a kid was respected if he wanted to work and the people in our area expected him to lie about his age. When I turned up at the railroad section house and asked for work the foreman asked how old I was. An eighteen-year-old; a blond fuzzy faced kid, who looked more like fourteen than the barely sixteen he actually was, told the automatic and expected lie. He asked me who I was. In the tiny place where we lived the grown-ups all knew each other. I told him who my step father was and he said for me to come in Monday and to bring some gloves and a lunch. I actually felt like I had arrived.

I was expected to work. My uncle was one of three farmers who worked together to put up all of their hay. I drove the stacker horse for them, starting when I was nine and during the summers for a few years, finally and proudly driving my uncle's new tractor at ages twelve and thirteen.

Three of us were talking, once, in the control room at CPS. As it worked out we were all born in Wyoming. Johnny said that he had never finished high school.

Fred replied "Well, you dumb son of a gun, why not?" Then he added, "Of course, I didn't either."

I had to make it unanimous. None of us had graduated from high school. I quit at fifteen but, for all of that, was making more than $80,000 a year in the eighties.

I have worked for anything that has ever come to me, have never wanted anything from any system and have never asked until this rotten situation came into my life. Getting unemployment after the debacle with B.P. was both a kick on the hind-end and a slap in the face, for me. In point of very relevant fact, I wasn't malingering while a bunch of hospital people were carrying me into a Canadian emergency room.

For some reason people had been trying to tie my symptoms to reflux. Allison says "he belches a lot." Anyone reading his report would get an impression that I was gross, not just twisted and sick. From what I have been told belching would be a symptom of reflux, which is a common thing and might help to shunt observation from the water issue. I very seldom belch. It's not polite and mostly not needed. Dr. Allison never did see or hear me belch. I was taking the medication given me by that aggressive doctor, even though I had told him I didn't have the symptoms he was describing. The consultants asked if I was on any medications and I told them. This may have been a spring board for what he said in the EME report.

Dr. Allison said I had reported being the only coworker with a Workers' Compensation claim.

Dr. Weldon had provided an extensive list of things he felt were probably contamination related. At the end of those, possible health risks for the future were addressed. Part of what he wrote was "… many if not most of (my) symptoms should resolve with loss of continued hydrocarbon ingestion. I have no doubt that there are some problems associated with this ingestion which may well persist…" Ample and detailed pages of commentary, which followed, spoke of various body systems and things that would likely continue, with probable down-stream effects. The EME report of this was that Dr. Weldon had said my symptoms should resolve with cessation of the exposure (if it existed).

During the examination something new was asked. Did I have any numbness in extremities? My toes had this at times, so it was volunteered. According to Dr. Allison, my socks were too tight. Also, there is a thing that some people have, I had one and didn't think much about it, during the interview. The morning after this though, waking up, something was remembered. This was that my fingers and toes often went numb when I slept. At times they felt like they were dead. Usually this was mostly on the left side. On this particular morning all of the fingers and toes were affected. They felt like wilted carrots, no feeling at all. I don't know what any of this is about but Dr. Allison did ask, so it probably means something. I didn't wear my socks to bed or on my hands.

Dr. Thorner's work was most memorable. According to her, I seemed to be a mental basket case. Being as messed up as this lady seems to have thought I was it's a wonder I didn't just starve to death. However, I was "able to get some training…" This sort of slant was seen throughout.

(1996) I was sent by a property management company to build a set of stairs in a warehouse leased by the U.S. Department of Fish and Wildlife. The stairs came out great. An elephant could have probably gotten up and down safely. The local head of this agency was looking at them. He said they really looked good and appeared to be solid. "That's important," he said, if someone fell on them we could be sued." Then he got a sour look and said "Litigants, you can't be too careful about litigants. We've had a few of them. It took ten years or so to get them off our backs; they're nuts, just nuts." Then, he said it again, as if for emphasis; "they're nuts, just nuts."

We were about the same age and had gotten along well during this project. He was talking to me as if we were on the same page. I felt fear for my job but this could not just be let to pass, he was talking to the wrong guy. "I'm a nut," I said. "It's been a few years since I fell out with my company. They have a stack of papers that say I have mental problems but it's not true."

He looked at me quietly for a moment and then spoke. "I know it," he said, "We all know it. It's how we handle situations. The Russians used to send people to asylums. I guess the message is don't make us do it to you." There was almost a little smile, then, as this head of a U.S. government office said "It doesn't matter how good an employee the person was or what his position was, either."

I met a lady from Anchorage and we were talking. As it turned out, her husband was well-placed in the Alaska Workers' Compensation system. She seemed to have been rather proud of that. She said that they (Apparently, the Comp people) had "had a meeting" and that, after this meeting, "the workers had it worse."

My son and I were installing some kitchen cabinets for a man who asked about my constant throat clearing. When he was told the story, this man said he hoped it never happened in his organization and that it would be the end of his career. This turned out to be the head of a small local government agency. He said he knew what was expected of him but could not do it because he was a practicing Christian.

I was helping a crew do some work on a man's roof. He came up there and was talking to us. My throat clearing was noted. He asked about it and was told the story. This turned out to be a retired person who had sold his business. There had been around a hundred employees.

He said "You fight it if you can."

In the early days of the job Larry Motz and I were flying together. He said there were things about his job he didn't like and that there were times when he was tempted to quit. (2009); I just remembered a time, on the plane, when Larry was talking. He spoke of some situation and said, a little bit ruefully, "They dumped the whole load on them; punitive and all." I had no idea, at the time, what he was talking about.

Every one of the EME's people answered the canned questions from the state in the same way. Apparently there was no industrial exposure. <u>Nothing relating to anything that had to do with me, had anything to do with anything that had to do with B.P.</u>

Text included with the report was interesting. It pointed out that the opinions expressed were those of the doctors and not of the medical consultants. I suppose these doctors were probably independent contractors and can easily see why. The test administered by Doctor Thorner was supposed to tell a lot of things about me. Still, going in, there was a statement.

"Test results are normal on patients who are in the early phases of assessment or psychotherapy because of emotional discomforts or social difficulties. Respondents who do not fit this normative population or who have inappropriately taken (the test) for non clinical purposes may have distorted reports. To optimize clinical utility the report highlights pathological characteristics and dynamics rather than strengths and positive attributes." (I would probably have said "assumed and/or alleged" pathological...)

All of this seems, to me, to fit into the "They'll paint you as a nut" prediction of that lawyer. In the next paragraph is found "The test cannot be viewed as definitive." Apparently, nobody wants to be held accountable in the event that one of their cases backfires.

Chapter Twenty-Three
The Next Step

The board was petitioned. I asked them to throw this thing out and not to let anyone who had anything to do with it have any input into my case. My request was long, using several examples of what was wrong including at least one very specific and very obviously purposeful lie (There was another, related to it and, together, they were almost comical). Also asked, was that if the report did survive, I be given a Second Independent Medical Evaluation (SIME). The company's attorneys came right back with every reason the report should stand. They did not feel that there was any reason for a SIME and tried to have Dr. Weldon's material thrown out, too.

Workers' Compensation Division's people didn't seem to be interested in irregularities or even in outright lying. The board decided to let the EME report and Dr. Weldon's material both stand. Definite conflicts were seen in them. There would be a SIME. It was to be with Dr. Paul Steer, in Anchorage. I wrote to him. On the day this was to be mailed, though, a letter arrived from Workers' Compensation. It advised me that I could bring nothing to the examination and could discuss nothing, either, except within certain parameters.

I learned that this was not to be a fresh look at the case as I had supposed. It was a review of the existing material, including that report from Seattle, and was just a rehashing of the stuff already in place. More; the SIME was my idea. This meant that it would become part of my evidence. (Which was something that I did not understand at the time.)

A lot of time had gone by with a lot of water under the bridge. It felt great to be back in Anchorage, though. There were memories and feelings here. I love the place. I visited with family members and enjoyed being back in Alaska.

Dr. Steer seemed like a nice person. He asked questions and did a very cursory examination. For the most part, nothing that was done could have said much of anything about the injuries I had, especially if they weren't acting up at the moment. Dr. Weldon had not done this little drill and that's what the company's attorneys used in trying to have his report thrown out.

One thing Dr. Steer did do was to listen to my lungs, having me breathe deeply. I was fine at the time and this could probably not have found anything, anyway. Years later, I would find that even an X-Ray wouldn't do the job. There is a more sophisticated rig that does, though, and the problem was and is, real. Steer told me that he sees people like me a few times a year. He said he only sees them *on appeal.*

It's the 2nd of May, 2008. I have heard from one of the guys. He had a bout with cancer in 1996 and lost a kidney, but is a survivor.

My first morning back in the South-48, after the Dr. Steer experience, I woke up with all of my fingers and toes numb. There is no idea what, if anything, this might have had to do with the water but I still suppose that there is something here, because of what Dr. Allison said in Seattle.

Dr. Steer's report, to my mind, was what it had to be; another disaster for me. The closest thing to favorable was "The only system complex that I think could be related, even remotely, to contaminated water, either through chemical or microorganisms, would be the diarrhea … a remote possibility rather than possible, probable or likely."

More typical of this man's input was "At no time (have I) ever had objective physical findings that were compatible with any known specific syndrome related to a known specific occupational toxin exposure." That statement is in conflict with a huge amount of credible input from well placed people, which this doctor had before him. He commented about Dr. Weldon's reported findings with expressions of doubt, saying that even my most active proponent admitted it was a theory at best.

Anyone who reads the Weldon report might react to Dr. Steer's comment. It is the report that Dr. Allison said he admired. Dr. Weldon did say that certain things were speculative. Also, he echoed Dr. Martin's assessment about the tank being a poor cracker. However, he was quite firm in his evaluations and noted that he did not doubt there might be significant amounts of various chlorinated hydrocarbons and other things involved; he used some long words. His report was very definite in assigning my problems to the water's contamination and this was his area of expertise.

There is not, nor ever was, anything alleged by me that was not found in these reports and did not square with what I had experienced personally. The CDC material was every bit as strong, evidence wise, as Dr. Weldon's report was. In some instances it went well beyond that. Neither the EME team nor Dr. Steer commented about the CDC material.

Both that material and Dr. Weldon's report addressed something called hypersecretory diarrhea. It is had in some situations, like Cholera. Dr. Weldon tied it to problems with our water. Dr. Steer said that it was "probably functional." He made no mention of the fact that this wretched mess lasted for nearly a decade and cleared up suddenly, completely and exactly, when the air line was removed. The scabby looking rash on my knuckles did not seem to be considered and drew no comment.

According to input from other professionals the diarrhea, the rash and various other things, demonstrated symptoms that are known to be associated with the possible-to-probable contamination involved.

Dr. Steer seemed interested in the numbness of my extremities, which I had never reported to anyone and have only written about here, in considering Dr. Allison's question to me about that. It was explained. The toes (manifested only during sleep) were said to be because of degenerative low back problems (I did not have back pain).

From the mid to later nineties on, the deadness that used to come on with sleep has gone. Now, the toes are always numb. Day or night, week in week out, year after year, they are numb. I would have thought that this would mean no feeling, like it used to be, but no. Numbness is now a kind of gross feeling, like I've been wearing wet socks for a month and the toes have swollen into each other. They can even hurt, and the feeling persists. It feels lousy, sometimes, when my toes rub the bed sheets. During the past several years one of the toes on my left foot hurts at times and, because of this numbness, I can't tell which one it is or even if it is only one.

As far as back problems are concerned, during the early seventies I built a lot of houses and did all of my own framing. This was when nail guns were just coming in and I still preferred my hammer to the new stuff. I carried a tool-belt with a 32 oz. framing hammer and two big bags of nails on it. Up ladders, on roofs, (etc.), those bags were hanging on my waist. It got to where my low back was tender. The first page on the very deep pile of paper I saw in Seattle was a report of the one and only time I saw a doctor about that and it had been years before. Going back to power plant operating saw the end of such things.

Dr. Steer must have had that page in his mind and, like everyone else seems to have done, apparently did relatively little examination of the file, which Dr. Allison said was the biggest of those he had ever seen.

In 2000, a blood clot was found in my leg. My doctor noted that the leg was swollen, too, and put me on water pills. That reminded me of two things. One was the minor incident at work where a medic had me sign the paper that apparently ended up on the Workers' Compensation Division people's computer. His report noted that my leg was swollen and speculated if I might have Phlebitis. The other thing remembered was Dr. Allison's assertion that my socks were too tight. Being a doctor and all, I would think that he would recognize something a PA could spot. That might be especially true, since only the right sock was too tight. I have had to go to the little socks that don't come up onto my ankles.

According to Dr. Steer my fingers were being affected by carpal tunnel syndrome, in this case, though and apparently, only when I sleep. There had been an operation for that in the mid eighties. The condition was said to be *recurring*. I don't feel any of this and remember well, what it felt like. (2008) I still have no recurring carpal tunnel symptoms. My fingers have stopped being numb.

Doctor Steer, like everyone else, had some facts scrambled up. Some of his logic, too, seemed to be based on things which were very short of accuracy. One of those seemed, to me, to be something-or-other (?) on Dr. Allison's part, in the EME report. According to him, from what I read, most of my symptoms came on during the time after the change of the water system. I see that idea as being highly inaccurate and rather strange, at best. I can't even imagine anything for it to have been based on. Along with many other things, this had been reported to the Workers' Compensation Division people. Like everything else reported to them, too, it wasn't even acknowledged. Instead of seeing that this was patently ridiculous and not knowing it had been reported as being such, Dr. Steer picked up on it.

He said that if there actually had been a problem, other people would have been affected. Apparently what my old doctor said didn't make it in. Also apparently, my comments to Dr. Allison, as it was with Dr. Christian, were not brought forward either. There has not been any acknowledgement of my reports about other people and, I suppose, never will be.

When the latest of our guys, Fred, died I called the other man that I knew had experienced the weird diarrhea, to tell him what had happened. George said that he could have helped when the company was fighting me so hard but knew (very well, I think) that they would have dumped him. He finally got the retirement I believe the company shafted me out of. George told me about the cognitive problems he was having and I told him the name of the stuff I was taking. I know of one more of our guys who is having the cognitive problems but don't know if he had that weird diarrhea or not.

George talked about going back into the mechanical room during the 1987 cleanup of the water tank and commented about watching a man emptying pans of oil and sludge into plastic bags. George hadn't remembered who this was but I know. He is the one who commented about it in the break room and who became one of our cancer victims.

After Fred died, I called the plant at Prudhoe Bay and talked to my old alternate. He told me the fellows had been on bottled water for years and only used the company water, now, for flushing toilets and so forth. They have not hooked the old air line back up. Interestingly, though, on another call a new guy told me the water fountain is still in place. The water tastes good and the hot water side is great for making tea (like George used to do).

If the state's people had taken me seriously there are now five people that I know of who might have had their cancer detected in time to make a difference and four of those are dead. I have had two tries at the offices of Attorney Generals and approached three governors. The closest thing to actual comment was when Ms. Bomenegan finally said that mine was "a dispute with my employer, nothing more."

According to Dr. Steer's report none of the contaminants, should they have existed, affected any "pre-existing condition," either. This is, ostensibly, covered by the Workers' Compensation laws. Apparently, the deviated septum was not affected, even though two doctors had commented about it. Dr. Steer felt that, since the "majority" of my symptoms had persisted after the alleged exposure ceased, evidence was against the water having been causative. Other symptoms moderating or going away was not mentioned, either. Problems that endure today and/or at the time of my visit to Dr. Steer are just a part of the whole. Along with that, Dr. Weldon wrote of things that he thought "might well endure." Some have.

As it turned out, the Steer report was open to cross examination. I had been told to send everything to Workers' Compensation and wrote a letter to Dr. Steer, which asked important questions. A lot of time went by. Nothing was happening while I thought Dr. Steer was aware of what had been asked. In one of those telephonic pre-hearing calls, though, I learned what nobody wanted to tell me. The letter was to have gone to Dr. Steer, which was a surprise. My questions had not been forwarded and I had not been advised.

The questions were rewritten and I got a letter from the doctor. He said he had been doing these evaluations for many years and I was the first person who had questioned his opinions. This man said he would be glad to answer my questions for four hundred fifty dollars an hour, cash in advance.

Chapter Twenty-Four
Way Of The World

After my visit to Dr. Steer I happened to meet a fellow in the Sears parking lot in Anchorage. He had a neat little mini motor home and I asked him what kind of mileage it got. We started to talk and conversation led to who we each were and so forth. My reason for being here was offered. I tell everyone and, if I live long enough, will tell the world. He had to tell me about his experience with the Veteran's Administration. One ear was completely useless, a mess up by VA's medical people. There was no hearing in it, at all. Trying to get some help with his problems, he was essentially told to buzz off. When this man persisted, he got a letter that commented about his possible mental condition. "Everyone knows what these people do," he said. "I decided that I could hear with just one ear." He said he wasn't about to get tangled up in that.

This takes me to the Alaska Medical Association. Efforts were made with about everyone. That included them. A doctor's letter to the AMA came to me with material provided through the comp procedures. Its comments showed one of the doctors in a rather revealing light. I wrote, again and again, to AMA, with no answer. Finally, one did come through, saying this doctor had done nothing wrong.

In August, 2006, I got a call from my doctor. Results of a CT scan on my lungs were in. Apparently there is something in them and I am being sent to a specialist. This lung thing has been going on for a long time and I have asked, repeatedly, for help. Several doctors, including Dr. Steer, have listened to my lungs without seeming to hear anything. Two have x-rayed them, without results. That lady at Harborview told me that I could prove nothing and declined to use proper diagnostics. People in Arkansas said they could not become involved. Workers' Comp doctors didn't appear to actually be interested.

All of that was long ago and I'm on medicare now. My doctor said that if something was going on in there it could become serious as I get older. The discomfort in my chest seems to be becoming less and less intermittent and more and more noticeable. Finally, this C.T. scan… (September, 2008); A cold has settled into my chest and it hurts in a way that I haven't experienced before.

I had requested that the original EME report be thrown out but that was denied. One day, something hit me like a sack of rocks. It was about Dr. Allison of the EME team. He seemed to have been vaguely familiar and had commented about not seeing Dr. Martin's report. Apparently, he knew him. The light came on when I wasn't even thinking about it. It was about that old building in Seattle with two doctors setting behind a counter. One of those was Dr. Martin. Memories can be vague but I found myself thinking that the other one was Dr. Allison.

Workers' Compensation was asked for reconsideration. The EME report was flawed, Dr. Allison had prior knowledge of my case, (etc.). This request was also denied.

Chapter Twenty-Five
What I learned Through Walt

Another memory eventually popped up. I didn't know where Walt was living. His brother was known to me but I hadn't even thought about that. I made a phone call, got the needed information, and made contact. Walt and I talked and then exchanged letters. Through them, information was received and realizations were had. The extra filter and faucet were installed by the guys before I got there. They had taken that on themselves because, even back then, the water tasted "off." Oil film was an item with some of them and they had known about it all along. The supervisors, especially, were aware of it.

Walt made it all clear. Something else was becoming clear, too. Report assertions were, I both believe and allege, near-to-complete misinformation and/or disinformation.

A copy of a letter from Walt was sent to Workers' Compensation. Before long a letter came from Mr. Wagg, the company's new attorney. He wanted to cross examine Walt. Among other things said was that he wanted to inquire as to Walt's "state of mind." My reply to Mr. Wagg and to the board was that it was alright with me but I objected to the mental connotation.

In the process of discovery after Walt's letter was submitted, I asked for a copy of the work order that had resulted in our water system being changed. Also asked for was the Plant Modification Request (PMR), which had caused it to be issued and all of the paper-work involved in the change. I got a copy of Walt's original job request and nothing more. It, though, is a clearly worded, direct, specific and straight forward request for the company to do something about the oil in our drinking water.

Walt was the man who wrote the request behind the change of our water system. That job request was the "smoking gun." It was absolutely and totally about oil in our drinking water. Apparently none of this meant anything to anyone and it has never even been acknowledged.

The company said they couldn't find the PMR or any more paper work. Getting this job request with its direct statements, in my opinion, might have been a collective fumble on the parts of the defending folks. It may have been, too and though, that time had gone by and some people at BP were not familiar with the case. There had been another attempt at discovery in 1993. The work order was asked for, then, too. It could not be found.

In 1999, thinking about the things Walt had told me, another realization was had and more was written on this book. I actually doubt that there is or ever was a work order. Walt's job request is what caused the PMR to come into existence. That should have created a work order, which would have gone on record, received a number for accounting purposes, been budgeted for, called for the ordering of material and the scheduling of work, (etc.). BP is a huge and very formal organization. Any job is done in keeping with procedure and is first rate.

This one was different, though. I believe it was done under the table and that the PMR was not followed through with because the brass knew this could become a hot potato. An old water pressure tank came from one of the other facilities. It was in bad shape and had to be brazed before it could be used. It was, however, not on any of the supply operation's books. Considering BP's level of professionalism, this seems exceptional at best.

According to log book entries the tank was installed by on-duty plant operations personnel, whose activities were routine and were not accounted for beyond just being on duty. Neither our maintenance department nor any contractors were involved. Significance of these things had not even crossed my mind.

The result, in my opinion, was that there was no paper trail, except for notations in an obscure supervisor's log book about a (numbered) PMR that is missing and never acknowledged.

Chapter Twenty-Six
Who Knew What?

Larry Motz and Bob Hartzler were setting out in the day area, on a rotation day, doing their weekly "handover;" exchanging department information from the outgoing man to the incoming one. I walked by and Larry spoke to me. He said they were just paper shufflers and didn't know about water and pipes and things of that sort. It would be years before another light came on for me and I may or may not see what I do suspect.

Every day the supervisors from each facility came together for a meeting at camp. What was going on in each man's area of responsibility was gone over. I believe that a person from HR was always there. It may be, too, that he was involved in discussions, or had at least been briefed, about the water's implications. When the light finally came on I remembered a detail from the time I had told Larry that I wanted to keep this as quiet as possible. "We can't do that," he said, "the exposure is too great. Think how many people have drunk the water there. Even the men at (security) check point one get their water from CPS." They carried their drinking and coffee water from the plant in 5 gallon plastic "Jerry" cans. This comment, about the men at the check-point, was made before there could have been a briefing.

I recall a time, in the control room, when I was talking to Jay and some others about my diarrhea and suspicions of the compressor's having contaminated our water. Fred had been a supervisor and gone back to operator status. He was on duty and spoke, saying there hadn't been any air involved for a few years. My reply was "Except for taking on water, when we pressure up the tank in order to blow out the fill line." Fred said we don't do it that way. When I said I did it that way, an interesting situation came up. My alternate was working a hold over and was standing at the back of the room. He said "I do it that way, too." Jay and Fred looked at each other in a quiet eye to eye; neither commented further.

I may be slow at that. Writing on this book started in early 1993. The time just mentioned was remembered in October, 1999. Fred retired to a small place near here. I saw him occasionally in Spokane. He once said that as far as he knew, I was the only one who had been hurt. I asked him where he thought all of the cancer among our guys came from. He died soon after this, from the effects of his.

In my opinion, after discovery of Walt's request, the water report and Dr. Christian's report as well, suddenly stood clearly and starkly exposed. So too, perhaps, does Dr. Christian's comment about something that happened "three years ago." Nobody seemed to care or even notice. Today I wonder how a company could work at sincerely investigating an alleged situation without finding a job request that was directly on-subject. I also wonder how the state could be so uninterested.

In absolute certainty, the old CPS water system had significant microorganism problems. It also had very significant chlorinated hydrocarbon problems and both are obvious, in hindsight. I believe that the cancer among our crew members is a direct result of the chemicals. I also state, clearly, that there are not and never have been, any rational explanations offered, which lead toward any other conclusions. If I am wrong, let someone say why I am wrong.

Chapter Twenty-Seven
A Serious Message To Deaf Ears

The big clean-up and change, of 1987, which was alleged to be about just doing away with a pressure vessel, was about oil in the water. It was after this change that the really bad episodes of harsh taste and bad smell came along. Those happened because of fifteen years of continuously building microscopic colonies in the water system. Those colonies may have become the most prevalent in the new charcoal filters of 1987. If there had been a third episode, it would have come on sooner and been worse. The system would have eventually become completely unusable.

Attempts to solve the problem with chlorine were futile because the little critters were of the tough customer variety that can live in a chlorine environment. They lived on hydrocarbons; chlorine would not have helped that, either, being a part of the situation. Doing away with the air line, flushing things out and changing to different filters, did away with all of it.

As far as the PMR and other related material not being located goes; the company's record keeping would rival that of the federal government. The idea of something as significant as a Plant Modification Request being lost is questionable, at best. Its number is recorded in a log book and I have copies of those pages. The details are in the log sheets, too, along with names. I have copies of all of it. No one cares but me; a seeming near-idiot because, in my opinion, of the *exposure* I represent.

I challenge BP, here, now and openly, to produce the PMR and to account for the scenario surrounding it. I also challenge the state of Alaska to investigate this matter and to prosecute British Petroleum if that is appropriate. I also challenge them to investigate the current Workers' Compensation system and discipline anyone whose actions might call for that or might *have* called for it.

The entry about the PMR is the work of a very sincere and honest supervisor. John kept meticulous records. The name of a company man who was sent to address the problem is on the record, too. Both names are there to be seen. John lives near here. I see him occasionally. Once, in a store, he said that he sure hoped I was wrong. No, John, I am not wrong or even close to wrong. You and I both know people that I believe have been sickened and even died because of that water. If I am wrong or even just off-base in any of this, let someone prove it, come close to doing that, or even provide a relevant thought in that direction.

The burden of proof is said, legally, to be on the company. Go for it, guys. I'm all ears and would like to hear some relevant information about something other than my mental condition. Maybe we are looking at *Workergate*.

I complained to the Workers' Compensation Division people about not getting the material requested in the discovery process and got a thing back from them, which said that if someone did not co-operate with discovery they could not enter material into evidence, which surrounded the subject involved. That would seem to be quite a prize for someone, if they wanted to hide something. I remembered that lawyer's comments about what this was all about. He had said "We're not as bad as Louisiana but almost."

My earlier attempts at discovery had tried to get copies of the superintendent's (Ben's) log book entries. Of interest were those surrounding the change to instrument air pressure made by Walt's crew and the changing back to design configuration, which was ordered by Ben. The company said, then, that the books contained *proprietary information*. This was alleged, I guess, to mean that they contained information too sensitive for a man to see, who had spent more than sixteen years intimately connected with a very low key operation. More likely, in my opinion, is that they would be too interesting to a guy who had lost his job for telling the truth. Probably even more likely, is that they would have exposed a lot of stuff where the company's case was concerned. These log-book entries were actually subject, ostensibly at least, to a legally mandated discovery process.

The more recent attempt also asked for Ben's material. This time, it could not be found. My comment to the state, in rebuttal to the original proprietary comment, was that I have had secret clearances from both the Air Force and the Navy. This was not meant to say anything except that I believed the company was being ridiculous and the state was helping them to break the law.

This material would probably have documented the presence of oil in our water, people's awareness and concern about it and a previous reporting of the situation, all of which were either denied or ignored in two very troubled reports. When O'Niel said that nothing came across with the air, he was not only wrong but out of order. People could know if something did come across (and some did know that) but could not possibly know if anything did not come across. When Dr. Christian said there had never been a report of oil in the water, a person can only imagine what went into that comment or what was left out of it.

I happened to be looking at some material received from the CDC, early on. It had to do with possible contamination related injuries. One description is of *aspiration into lungs during oral ingestion*. This is about *sever pulmonary injury* and is one which troubles me. I actually believe the diarrhea probably helped me, where my digestive tract is concerned. The lungs, though, might be another matter. Problems there can be painful and dying from them is said to be a hard way to go. Whatever is going on there is felt more and more, as I grow older.

Other entries touched on *pretumor diseases, chronic bronchitis, anacid gastritis, ailments of the larynx and skin*. This spoke of lung cancer in males and other things along with that, in females. Also included, besides lung, were *larynx and skin cancer in males*. Still another entry concerned situations directly connected to *contamination of water by impurities such as petroleum oils*. This had to do with *a high prevalence of esophageal cancer*. One which followed was about *a clear cut history of chronic intake of an oily substance*. This was about carcinoma and the prognosis was said to be poor.

Believing that the people on the company side of this were acting dangerously, I wrote to Workers' Compensation Division. They were asked to consider these things. Also, I thought about how my wife and I have had to let our life insurance go because we cannot afford the premiums. A letter was received from Mr. Wagg. It said:

> I think your letters indicate a recognition that the evidence is overwhelmingly on our side in this case. (Actually, there was a helpless recognition that the power was overwhelmingly on their side; the physical evidence is and always has been totally in my favor.) I would note in reviewing the medical records that it also seems there is not much in the way of medical treatment that you have previously required or that you will require in the future. Given that the only issue remaining open to be tried by the board concerns past and future medical care, it would seem to me that we might be able to work out some solution to this case which does not require a full fledged hearing. I would be interested in your thoughts on what BP and their insurer could reasonably do to satisfy your requests for medical care. Given again, that there does not appear to be much in the way of medical care that you could arguably say is work related, it may be that we can work out a solution that allows you to get any needed medical care, and yet does not require tremendous expenditures of time and money on both our parts in getting this claim resolved by the board.

When Mr. Wagg first assumed the role left to him by an out-going legal office, there was a pre-hearing. Out of the blue, on the phone, he had something to say. "You could drop your case, the company has put a lot of money into this already." He seemed to be personally committed to something that simply turned up on his desk.

It took two efforts to answer Mr. Wagg's letter.

My thought was and is straight forward; reinstatement.

There is much that has been done improperly in all of this. Wrong could be set right. Practical concerns could be addressed. There are health problems. There are also some risks for the future. Both were caused by what I said they were caused by; the old CPS water system. It's all well enough documented. As long as diagnosis is hindered and possible treatment cannot be directed at the cause, there can be no actual help for me. The process that has been brought to bear stands between me and that…

Another letter followed this one, which challenged his various assertions. It also described much of how I saw what was happening. That was not flattering but was, I believe, very true. It is my belief that the thing is completely unworthy. He was told about my feelings. When the company wanted to proceed in good faith, I said, I was waiting to hear it.

During one of those telephonic pre-hearings Mr. Wagg and the lady from Workers' Compensation Division, Ms. Gaal, were after me to go to hearing. I hadn't even known there was to be such a thing. With that realization in place, though, it wasn't too hard to see where this was going. I told them I could not win and believed it was engineered to be that way. I also told them there was one thing that could be done. Wagg asked what it was and I told him about writing a book and intending to publish it.

Before long a letter came to the house. It was from Mr. Wagg. He said the board preferred that we proceed informally, when possible. He asked me, by way of discovery, to forward a copy of my "book" to him as soon as possible and, in no case, more than thirty days. The quotation marks were his.

My reply was that, if he was really interested in "discovery," he should read his files. This time, the quotation marks were mine. Another letter came right back. It had what seemed to be some legal terms and a few "(so and so) vs. (so and so)" references. Apparently, this was some sort of legal apparatus. It demanded that he be sent all discs, notes, back up discs, (etc.). *I wondered if I was allowed to keep anything for myself.* The impression had, was that I was not.

Actually, I could not comply, even if I had been willing to do that. This was more of an idea than a work in progress. What I had was highly unorganized and was just a few notes scattered around in various discs that were used with my old word processor. Separating it out of those and into hard-copy would have been fruitless and very difficult. As far as the discs were concerned, the processor was an obsolete model of an obscure make. No other machine could read my discs. Sending them away would do nothing for anyone. Some years later I asked an attorney friend what this was all about. He said "Tell the guy that this is America and to pound salt."

Chapter Twenty-Eight
The Hearing

The great day had to come and it finally did, on the fifteenth of January, 1997. Five years and eight months after my report of a safety problem to Larry Motz, the thing was about to come to a head. A new world had been discovered and experienced during that time. It was one whose existence I would have never even imagined.

Arrival at the Anchorage office of the state's Workers' Compensation Division was before their people came to work. I sat in a hallway, on a chair, reading and making notes, with papers piled around me on the floor. A lady came in and said I could go to the hearing room and use a table. That was done and I sat there going over material. There wasn't a clue about what was going to happen but I wanted to be as ready as possible.

After awhile, leaving the room, I passed a woman in the hallway. "Is something wrong in there?" she asked, "it sounds like someone is sick, in the hearing room. I had been setting there coughing, choking and clearing my throat. It had been going on for years. During the eighties Jay used to say that he could tell who was approaching his office by the way they sounded. "Here comes Merv," he would say, "clearing his throat." People are always offering me advice or their favorite cold remedies. This has slowed down in recent years but it was bad yesterday (in October, 2009).

The hearing was presided over by Mr. Jaquot. He seemed, to me, to be awfully young to be in such a position. This man had spoken to me on the telephone (nothing in writing, of course) about the upcoming hearing. I was told that there would only be two issues addressed. One was if there was something wrong at work. The other would be if it had hurt me. He said "If anything else is brought up I'll shut your hearing down." I suppose this was with regard to my continuing assertions of company wrong doing and law breaking. None of that was ever going to be an issue.

There were two people on the board of this hearing. I got the impression that they were employed elsewhere and served on an as needed basis. They were S.T. Hagedorn and Patricia Volendorf. Mr. Wagg represented the employer. Another attorney, a company employee, sat beside him. Other people came and went. Apparently, the thing was open to the curious, who seemed to be spectators from the Compensation office as well as from the company, whose building was near-by.

Before the thing started I had a question for Mr. Wagg. "I suppose, regardless of where we each stand in regard to this, the project is to find out the actual facts?" He told the truth. "I'm employed by B.P."

The hearing was a formal type of thing. We went on the record and off the record, (etc.). The lawyer objected here and there. Things started off with Mr. Wagg's motion that the whole thing be thrown out. The board went off-record and left the room for awhile. Returning, their decision was to take the matter under advisement. We would proceed and see if anything else came up, which might reflect on the motion.

Next, there was objection to two of my witnesses. Their names had not been submitted in a timely enough fashion. One of those had seen the inside of the tank during the original clean-up. He was the man who took sludge out of it by the "pans full" and would later die of cancer. The other was Slim, who had experienced skin problems on his hands. It was pointed out to me that both of the witnesses denied me could be used as rebuttal witnesses, whatever that meant, I had absolutely no idea about what was going on.

Jim O'Niel had told me he would be a hostile witness, if subpoenaed. As it worked out, Ms. Gaal told me by phone that there wasn't enough time for a subpoena for him. Jim would not be available. There was nothing in writing. Also not available was George, who had experienced symptoms similar to mine. His name had been given to Dr. Christian, to never be heard of again. He told me that he had not been approached on the subject. He would not be available and let me know that, rather sternly.

Ben and his family were just flying out of Fairbanks on vacation. He agreed to call in when they landed and he could get to a phone. The board was advised about this. Instructions were given to the office to forward the call when it came in.

My permission for Mr. Wagg to quiz Walt turned out to be inadequate and my objection to the mental thing, irrelevant. I was to have (Somehow?) provided Walt to this lawyer, which was not, and is still not, understood and no one was about to tell me. The upshot was that Walt's letter would not be allowed into evidence. I had failed to cooperate with discovery.

For reasons not understood, the log book entries and, apparently, their overview were to become part of the record but would not be allowed into evidence on my side. Neither would Dr. Christian's report or its overview. They could be used, though, for cross examination (again, at the time; whatever that meant).

Mr. Wagg pointed out a 1993 decision by the board. It said that mine was a "complex" case. This turned out to be a legal term. Something about it threw my medical material out the window, as far as this hearing was concerned. Other things affected my ability to cross examine. (?) Along with all of this, a paper of some sort had either been turned in, allowed to stand, or (?), which made the only admissible medical material, for me, that of Dr. Jennifer Christian. The lawyer's comment at this point could not be disagreed with. He said this would be totally against my case.

Not having a clue about how this all worked and not being able to get any representation, direction, explanations or advice had its drawbacks.

I read my opening statement. Wagg did his. Mine described symptoms and the situation I believed was behind them. The other was what a person might have expected. After these presentations were finished, since there was no admissible evidence on my side, the time was turned to calling people on my witness list. Calls were put on a speaker phone so that everyone could hear them.

The original man from the A.D.E.C. was qualified as an expert witness. He had seen Mr. Wingerter's report but that was years ago. A copy was sent to him by FAX. Stated in his comments, was that the design of our water system would have been against safe practices. In answer to questions, he said the design as presently had, since 1991, was acceptable. Some of his comments, from my notes, were "...introduction of contaminants unacceptable... Not an approved technique... Potential or likelihood that the water is degraded... ... would not meet our standard."

(During a discussion about how things can be determined;) "Knowing is one way, laboratory is another. (Apparently saying that some things are simply known by qualified people). Rely on water quality... Historical precedence can be confirmation."

(Wagg) "No way to express opinion other than evidence... hypothetical? (Witness) "No, (use of) regular compressors is prohibited activity. Contaminant source is the key question." (Mr. Jaquot) "Is the A.D.E.C. report adequate?" (Witness) "I would have gone further... It is lengthy..." I recall this man's saying that the system had been in violation.

Skip, former operator at the water plant, was called. "Took tests for base line information... Figures loaded during good times, slowed down sampling during bad..." My memories of statements made by him about O'Niel's alleged way of handling data did not get into this. Mostly, when I asked questions, Mr. Wagg objected. It's hard for a lay person to ask much of anything; especially when he really doesn't know what's going on.

Henry had been away from Alaska for a number of years. As examination of his credentials was made I was surprised. He was or had been, on the water boards of two states and was then teaching water treatment at a university. He easily qualified as an expert. Asked about the A.D.E.C. report, he said "I questioned it when I read it." Included in his comments were some about times when my situation was discussed among the men at the water plant. He said that during one of those discussions the guys went into their computer. There were fifteen times when the chlorine residual at CPS was zero. For Henry to have remembered this detail, in such detail, after all those years, it must have seemed important to him.

With contamination being the key issue, the situation is highly significant. Contamination depletes chlorine. I don't believe that Mr. Wingerter knew about this. If he did, it was treated the same way my log book entries had been. As I said before; tests performed by the water department were such that they could not have picked up on what was happening at the plant. The chlorine residual problem probably should have rang alarm bells all over the water department but, for some reason, was not a part of their official records and was apparently ignored.

Henry said our facility was the only one having this problem. His comment was (I'm out of notes here) that the system was unacceptable. This highly qualified individual was very specific about the situation. Spoken of, was the taste of the water when he came to the plant. He said that it was like the "vilest swamp water." He also commented about the filters and how they had been installed wrong. Maybe this reflects on why they were green when Curley saw them (Had become strata for microscopic organisms?).

Johnny was what he had always been; funny. He talked about how the system was. "We were young back then," he said, "ten feet tall and bullet proof. Today, we're all fat and bald; we wouldn't stand for it." Everyone in the room laughed. He commented about the rash on his hands and thighs. It had cleared up when he was promoted. In his mind, at the time, this was because he didn't have to wash his hands so much. I pointed out that his promotion took him away from the plant and the water system. None of us knew the nature of our problem back then.

Jay was interesting to me. We had talked before this, in setting up the interview. He told me he did not want to participate but would cooperate, saying he would be a hostile witness since he didn't believe that I was harmed there. I told him what was felt; that I was sorry for what had happened. His reply was the same but, I think, in a little bit different direction. He said "I'm sorry, too, very sorry." Jay and I had talked a lot, over the years. We both felt that this was far more than just a job. Retirement, when it came, would find each of us looking back.

As far as my being harmed was concerned, I asked him if it was normal for a man to pass out behind the wheel of his car. He replied that it wasn't normal for a man to drive for three days without a drink of water. Jay had to be prodded on two occasions to address a water problem, which he was completely unaware of and refused to hear about. He would actually argue about it. All he would have to have done, either time, would have been to take a drink from the water cooler. The first time, he had finally done that. The second time, for some reason, he was determinedly holding out and it took a strong complaint from someone besides the crew to get even that concession. Jay is the person who argued with a man who was an absolute expert on the subject.

His own log book entries confirm the problem, mentioning both bad taste and smell, but even these realities are denied by logic he would eventually put forth in my hearing. Further, there cannot be a connection, in his mind, between my situation and the water, as witness his statement that he did not believe I had been harmed there.

Jay's ideas about my driving for three days without a drink of water are both absurd and completely irrelevant. A person will not pass out if they drive for three days without a drink of water. The idea doesn't apply to me, though, anyway. In the first place we were less than forty eight hours away from home when the incident happened. In the second place, I clearly remember my family and I being at a restaurant the evening before. This was around nine PM. The kids and I had a long winded discussion going and nobody was very anxious to get back into the van. We sat there talking, after our meal, drinking ice water. The waitress finally left us a pitcher of it. This was not the only time we stopped to eat, either. I drink water with my meals, usually more than one glass. I specifically remember stopping the day before this, too.

Also remembered, is buying some snacks and a bunch of Canadian fruit juice, later that day. Jay could not be told these things and the idea he has, seemed to be firmly fixed in his mind. I have to wonder if he thinks I drove for "three days" without five kids having a drink of water. Every time we stopped for gas it was refill time and the ice chest we carried with us had plenty in it, as well. We were no drier than his family might have been. I've driven the Alaska Highway more than a dozen times and have only lost consciousness behind the wheel there (or anywhere else) once in my entire life. I have never driven that or any other highway without taking a drink of water; or holding my breath, which would make about as much sense.

In testimony, Jay remembered the air line that had been used to pressure the water system. Apparently, though, he still didn't accept its implications. Asked (by Mr. Jaquot, I think) was if he had noticed a difference in the taste of the water after the change. He replied in the negative, showing, as I just wrote, that he even denies the realities recorded in his own log book. This recording must have been just a mechanical thing, in my considered opinion. Apparently he didn't actually accept the realities embodied in this, even as he wrote it, and the feelings that went with his version of reality were continuous.

A documented bad taste and smell, in response to complaints and personal tasting, resulting in a major effort/change, with no improvement? Jay ordered the work done. A person would think that a change in taste (and smell) would be a necessity. As the man in charge, he was the one who should have assured that there was an improvement. As for Mr. Jaquot; an absolute expert witness has described "the vilest swamp water." I would have supposed the salient point should have been what was said by the expert witness. I would also think that the no improvement comment should have revealed contradiction and aroused some interest.

One very memorable thing, for me, was the very good taste of the water after the repair. It was not only a dramatic change from the situation that had brought it about but a marked change from what had been experienced over time, as well. I doubt if anyone will ever have to use lemon juice to drink the water at CPS again. With the bottled water they are mostly drinking now, that's probably a certainty. The air-line's being disconnected, of course, makes that an absolute.

On my way home from the Dr. Steer experience, passing through the Seattle airport, I bumped into a fellow who had transferred to CPS after I was gone. We talked for a moment and I mentioned the water and my case. He was totally surprised, saying he had always thought I had just taken a separation package and left. Commenting about the water, he said "The water at CPS is very good."

(2002); I told Fred of Jay's comment about not noticing any improvement in the taste of the water after the repair. He said he really wouldn't know and that he probably didn't drink eight glasses of CPS water in fifteen years. That may be true but I worked a lot of shifts with him. He drank enough coffee during those years to sink the Exxon Valdez. Every bit of it had chemical contamination. (2007) I met him at the Fred Meyer store, here in Spokane. He had been operated on for cancer and lost his bladder. Fred had a bag under his clothes and said he was "weak as a kitten." He did say the doctors said they thought they "got it all." I hoped so. The saying on the job was that if you couldn't get along with him it wasn't his fault.

Fred's death is a big part of the push going on here as I try again, for the umpteenth time, to get the word out. It frosted me and I'm up to here with all of this. His wife said he never snapped back after the surgery. He was the fifth CPS cancer victim I knew of at the time. Later, I learned about the sixth and, then, found out about number seven, the survivor. A person has to wonder how many there may be out there but I don't know where people are.

Recently I tried to re-create a list of people, from memory, and finally came up with 56 names. That number is probably several short and I would say that it is around sixty, which would not include the security people at the check-point. I recall one man, years ago, who groaned and fainted onto the control room floor. The guys who were there said that he was probably on drugs.

John wasn't at home for his call but was supposed to have been. He wrote the log book entries about the PMR, the oil coalescent, etc. In setting up the interview he had said he didn't mind talking with me but that it would have to be cleared with the HR department.

Ben's call never did come in. Along with the man who was not available, this was three very important calls. Added to these would be the two witnesses who were disqualified because of my late request for them. I believe each of the five could have confirmed the presence of oil in our drinking water, even in significant amounts. I also believe that Jim O'Niel should have been provided to this hearing.

A continuation was requested so we could hear from the witnesses Mr. Wagg would allow. It was denied. Mr. Jaquot said I had had

"Years to prepare for hearing." If that had been centuries it would have made no difference. I was in a totally strange world and might as well have landed on Jupiter. We each read our closing statements. Mine expressed concern for what might become of me if I ended up with a hole in my throat, like my former coworker had. Could I do all of that throat clearing through one of those?

Mr. Wagg's comments were well planned and probably what a closing statement should have been. He said "We do not argue the existence of Mr. Eggleston's symptoms. They are too well documented. They may or may not be life threatening. However, they did not arise out of or in the course of, his employment." He said there might have been a little bit of oil in the CPS water but it was not enough to have the effect. I don't suppose that, legally, he needed to be qualified as an expert witness to make such a comment in a closing statement or to back it up with any information.

How much dirty lube oil is acceptable in a potable water system? We had gone from "It simply could not have happened" to this, one step at a time, as I furnished irrefutable but never acknowledged evidence, with no concessions except for this tightly worded closing statement. Its content says a few things to me. It is my belief that some members of the opposition had to have known at least something about the oil in our drinking water.

Mr. Wagg had provided everyone with copies of his documentation. Offered as evidence for the company but not allowed in it for me, were the very things I saw as being so problematic.

The "CPS Water Quality Report" sat there in all of its glory. I allege lies, inaccuracies, inconsistencies, manipulation, distortion, (etc.). Probably nothing in this report could stand up to scrutiny. Some of it might possibly turn out to have been purposeful fraud. Still, there would be no examination of it and, in this lifetime, will not be. My overview of it might as well have been used for fire starter.

A new thought has entered, in this most recent re-writing. The company's lawyers objected when I tried to submit this document and its over-view, to the state. I was just trying to tell my story and didn't know there would be a bunch of formal stuff up ahead. I had no idea that there was a regimented "their side and my side," at this point. They said it was written by some of my coworkers, which is what I saw as being deception. Likely, I suppose and perhaps, is that (1) my attempt to explain things didn't fit into the arrangement of procedures and (2) the report really wasn't an official document, since the hygienist made no real input to it. Certainly, the overview would not qualify.

When the company's lawyers entered the water report as evidence on their side, though, it went through like it was greased.

Dr. Christian's material was next. Little or no better, I allege, it was supremely safe from objective examination.

Barney's letter, which tells me to drop this and threatens discipline if I do not, is right there, too. It may have been straight up and screaming for attention evidence of harassment; which is said to illegal.

These, the EME report and Dr. Steer's material were all there. During the hearing the EME team, in Seattle, had been alerted and was waiting in the event that they were called upon to testify. A lawyer told me that companies and government agencies can buy anything they want. Individual motives and circumstances are not being evaluated here.

Chapter Twenty-Nine
How It Came Down

That evening, I was listening to Anchorage radio. Talk was political. First, it was about BP. Then, it was about the legislature. After that, it surrounded the company and the legislature. The program centered on the subject of tort reform. The idea there is, ostensibly, that something has to be done about "people who sue."

I had been waiting for the ruling from Workers' Compensation Division and would have liked to be able to get some medical help or, at the least, have tried to do that. I wasn't entertaining any great ideas, though. That hearing had left a bad taste in my mouth. The whole thing, from my report to Larry Motz on, seems to have been what I am now certain it was.

The letter came in on February 13th. It was a total ruling against me. I had "failed to prove (my) case from the preponderance of the evidence." The original attorney had told me that the burden of proof was on the company but, as far as I can tell, they never even approached the subject, except to deny it.

The water expert from ADEC had not disagreed with Mr. Wingerter's report. A member of that department himself, such a comment should not have been expected. What he did say was clear and sufficiently detailed enough to show the problem's existence. "Contamination… Violation…" The man had not backed down an inch, even if he was professionally discreet.

Jay did not notice a change in the water's taste after the system was repaired. In the face of an eye witness experts' testimony about "the vilest of swamp water;" before a needed repair ordered by Jay himself, documenting both bad taste and smell in the log book, this procedure based their position on Jay's highly problematic comment.

Noted, was Skip's saying test results could be skewed. Not mentioned, was that his testimony said they were horsed around with routinely. Also of no apparent significance to these people was Henry's reporting that there were fifteen times when the chlorine residual at the plant was zero and that our's was the only facility where there was such a problem.

Johnny (allegedly) said that his rash went away when he quit washing his hand so much. Actually, the ruling said that, not Johnny. What he did say was that, at the time, he had thought the rash went away because he had become a supervisor, not having to wash his hands so much. He also said you can't pressure up a water system with an air compressor but Mr. Wagg had that comment tossed out.

The board didn't seem to notice that both of our rashes cleared up under the same sort of situation; his when he left the exposure and mine when the exposure left me. They didn't note, either, that we both had the rash on more than just our hands.

In more than thirty years, I've known a lot of people from the maintenance side of power plant operations. I was there for a few years myself and used to wash my hands a lot, too. There is an old joke in the trade. It says that a power plant operator washes his hands after using the bathroom. The maintenance crew washes theirs before that. This very unusual rash had absolutely nothing to do with washing hands. It was totally unique to the time and place where our flawed water system was had.

During the fuss and harassment after the report of my problem I mentioned Johnny's rash to Ben. He told me Johnny had very dry skin. That's something I have lived with all of my life. I wonder if Slim had dry skin, too.

"We put substantial weight on the reports of the EME team and Dr. Steer." (Stand behind our people) That must have been true, I marveled at this one. Dr. Steer had made a list of things he was trying to tie my symptoms to. In the ruling, if I understood what was being read correctly, this became the list of things being alleged in my claim.

Postmark on the ruling was January 29th, two weeks before the thing arrived at my place. It said I had a right to appeal. That had to be done within a certain and ridiculously narrow time frame. Wording was a little bit vague. I couldn't decide if the clock started when they had sent this or when it was received. Going down to the post office, I asked about this letter. The guy behind the counter said that offices have postage meters. They postmark the letter themselves, but it goes out when they get around to it. I asked about the return receipt. "That, too," he said.

Two weeks seemed like a long time for a letter to take, in coming from Anchorage. Those letters had rained on me for years. A couple of days was the norm. I wrote an appeal. In it, I told these good folks that I had a certain amount of time to do this and the letter's delivery date was clear because of the return receipt. My effort was made quickly and pointed out some things. The EME report was a joke and some of its problems had been pointed out to them, before. Dr. Steer's was little, if any, better. Much had been pointed out to the board but none of it had ever even been acknowledged.

Time went by. One day my daughter had a message for me when I came home. A lady had called from Anchorage. Her message said that my appeal was too late. These people had written to me constantly, often about little or nothing. Something this significant would seem to have called for a letter to me; for their files, if nothing else. Apparently, though, the formal part of this would be a phone call but nothing in writing.

That lady from Harborview and her "nothing in writing" comment; the attorney general's office and their long silence; Barney's (probably illegal) verbal order; Ms. Gaal's telling me that Jim O'Niel would not be subpoenaed; Mr. Jaquot's warning about shutting down my hearing if anything not to his liking was brought up and, now, this telephone call...

As far as that message goes, the only woman I knew of at Workers' Compensation Division was Cathy Gaal. She had been dealing with me and had made comments (one of those in writing), which caused me to question her perceptions. She may or may not have been the woman on the phone. If that was the case, though, she might have had something to do with holding a predated letter until the last possible moment. At the very least, I believe, she should have been aware of its late arrival.

My daughter said she was told I could appeal to the Alaska state court system. I see this as being a bad thing. Besides being far beyond me, financially, the risks would be terrible and the results would have probably been catastrophic.

This seemed like the end of a bad thing. All that's left to do is what they have been trying to force on me, all along. Like Howard said about people that Sears jumped on; "Those people are out on their ear. All they have left is to bad mouth the company."

Chapter Thirty
Here's An Idea

Ben once said that in order to properly criticize anything you have to be able to present a workable alternative. Actually, the first one of those is for good company people, who recognize a problem, to be realistically allowed to step up to the plate and make things right. They cannot do that because of (1) the insurance industry, (2) the government and (3) higher-ups in their own organizations. People who have actually been hurt should never have to fight for their lives because of it but that seems to be the case. Probably worse, too, are things that are in place to help beat them up. All of this is what it may happen to be, but a genuinely frivolous or without merit case should be recognizable and properly dealt with.

Since we must be stuck in these "parallel legal systems" there may be ways to re-arrange them. With this in mind, a person climbs up a ladder, falls off and breaks his arm. There is no potential for liability to the company, which seems to be the simple criteria for what we see now. Neither the employer nor the insurer have any desire to fight this case. The employee is instructed at once, in written, simple and straightforward language, about particulars of the system. Failure to do this brings real world consequences.

Good faith on the part of the employer should never be assumed and bad faith should be both watched for and accounted for. Responsibility for dealing with a problem rests squarely and realistically on the employer, as it should. The state's Workers' Compensation

Division is notified within ten working days. Again, failure to do this brings absolute and tangible real world consequences. Our man goes to his own doctor. The bill is paid, lost time is compensated for and every one is where they should be.

Now, something is alleged to have happened and is reported to the company. They say "No way!" This will be contested. Report is made by the company, with copies to the employee, with no nonsense, no exceptions and no excuses, within five working days. The report must state that the company will be contesting the claim. If this is not all done, the company cannot contest the matter. If a company says that they will be doing that, the first thing that the state must and does do, is to investigate to determine (1) what and how much potential there is for liability to the company and (2) what the potential is for harm to the employee and to other employees. That project cannot be handed over to folks who are "approved" or in any other way, are tied to a jaundice or bias prone system.

It might be that an officer of the department can be a qualified individual who is dubbed an investigator. He is joined, initially and temporarily, by a representative of O. S. H. A and both people file reports. Those reports are each personally reviewed by the commissioner of labor, who will analyze the whole case upon completion of all procedures and write a summary and forward it to the governor. All of these reports would be left open forever; subject to examination and review at any time by interested people, whoever they might happen to be. They could be had as evidence in any situation, into perpetuity.

These things must be done before the thing can proceed, in any direction. If either/both potential for harm or liability are significant, special note is made of the situation and it is referred for observation to a representative from the governor's office, who must account for the entire matter as it goes along, watching for violations of the law and/or ethics. Reasons for, and investigation of, the potential for harm or liability go on record and are revisited occasionally if anything seems potentially noteworthy.

A special terror for companies is the prospect of being found "In violation." Larry once mentioned this word to me but I wasn't up to speed yet. B.P. absolutely was in violation, according to the ADEC man. I believe some of them knew it, after my report, or at least knew of the possibility that they had been in violation. With pressures from government agencies and insurance people it is understandable, if unfortunate, that I really did not have a job or a chance, after my report of the problem.

A government agency should not be able to tromp into some company's office and slap someone with a huge penalty because of an honest (If stupid) mistake. Government practices guarantee monstrosity against a victim. There are pressures on businesses.

Each and every communication regarding the alleged situation must be recorded and reported to the assigned hearing officer, with copies to the employee. Merely verbal, on subject, communications, if they are detected, brings accountability and the possibility of serious consequences.

It should be acknowledged that many companies or their management will cheat if they feel the need to and rationalize if they are allowed to. Laws and penalties do tend to scare employers, except for those who are powerful enough to spurn them. Government agencies can be high-flying, too, in two directions; they can both scare the pants off little employers and cozy-up to the big ones. Also, insurance companies are behind the scenes and are tough enough that employers, both large and small, fear them.

Back to our hypothetical case; everyone who is involved; the employee, a company man and the observer from the state, ought to be able to set down together. There should be no lawyers present, of any kind. A straightforward, real-world look can be had, with no implications or consequences for anyone. The state's man has to evaluate the situation and look at it for possible down-stream problems, including concerns about other employees. The door is always left open for future situations.

Both the potential and the reason for liability are noted, recorded and kept in mind. If agreement is possible and every issue properly addressed, including fear of reprisals (for the employee) or penalties (for the employer), agreement should be allowed and the matter settled. Even the state's man can get past implications, and waive penalties, of someone having been "in violation," where an innocent mistake has been made. **All of this, would be real-life tort reform.**

While the insurer is not physically represented, their role/reaction would be strictly observed. They are allowed no input and anything but total propriety is reported directly to the insurance commissioner. Any communication between the employer and the insurer about the situation must be copied to the insurance commissioner and there are teeth in the law. Penalties to all parties for misbehavior, at any point in the process, include both personal criminal prosecution, realistic fines for the company, and discipline for people in government offices, including possible prosecution.

A big company gets a big fine for actual misbehavior. This idea is not meant to hurt anyone, of course, but to let reality be felt and, consequently, to prevail. If there are no teeth in laws, there are not really any laws. Neither not reporting nor months long "sincerely investigating (not reporting)," are allowed for an employer. No "You wouldn't want for someone to go to prison, would you?" is available to the bureaucracy, either. I believe that Barney's letter to me should have been noted and addressed, as violation, by the bureaucracy.

Time is allowed for all parties to get their materials together. This is considered to have been done when each side believes that they are ready. It is all flexible and forgiving. Pressuring or abusing of the employee or impropriety on the parts of either the company or the state's people brings serious consequences and, if alleged, must be acknowledged, investigated and reported on. Actions of both groups are reviewed, then, by a representative of the attorney general's office, who must report the matter directly to the governor, who has recourse options.

I feel that the performance of the then-personnel in the State Workers' Compensation Division in Anchorage should be investigated.

Procedures are presented to the employee clearly enough that he or she knows what to look for and can call attention to what might seem, to anyone, to be amiss with either the employer or the state's people. No one, including the Attorney General's office can just bob along on a sea of "Nothing in writing." Communications between involved parties or agencies must be recorded and reported.

Actual and confirmed violation, by either the employer's people or the bureaucracy, at any stage of the proceedings, immediately awards to the plaintiff. Their portion is closed with no further questions. Violation is then dealt with as a separate matter. There are no statutes of limitation on these, what I believe have become and should be called, human rights violations. The violator's entire part in the original situation and the ethics problem as well, are then reviewed and reported to a separate committee. They deal with problems, if found, in either or both situations.

Penalties, there, include fines and punitive damages, the latter going to the victim of the abuse. Also, where appropriate, there should be individual criminal prosecution, which should look at both the company and involved individuals or agencies.

When things are ready there is a committee. As the voting portion of it, five members are selected like a jury might be, from the same list of people. Disqualifiers would be if a person has been involved on either side of a contested case before, if there has been close relationship with someone else who has been, or if there is admitted prejudice.

Instructions to this committee include the fact that this is about an employees' allegations of harm. They are to watch for details, ask questions, volunteer observations, discuss, participate, (etc.). They are to be interested, participating, cooperating and transparent. They are to try to have empathy with both the employer and the employee, neither of whom are to be abused or to miss anything that might be significant. Everyone is to be on the look-out for such things and under obligation to bring them forward.

In an improved Workers' Compensation Division scenario the true emphasis would be on and for actually injured workers, where there may be potential for real-world harm. There would be no lawyers and there would be no board. The people who saw my case sat there as Mr. Wagg threw my medical stuff out the window and stopped me from having people give their input. Those folks saw that I wasn't represented and heard things over the speaker phone that, in my opinion, should have raised the hair on the backs of their necks. They saw that I could hardly ask or present anything but signed a statement, which said I had failed to prove my case from the preponderance of the evidence.

The scan on my lungs called for a trip to another specialist, who interpreted what he saw on it and ordered a PET scan. This is, I think, supposed to see if the thing in my lungs is cancerous or not. Looking at the first scan, he showed me scars on my lungs and the swollen lymph gland, which was fairly large. I told him that there had been an industrial exposure. He looked right at me and, with a very sober and firm voice, said "I don't want to hear one word about that."

I challenge the State Workers' Compensation Division, in Anchorage, to produce that list. If they cannot or will not, I then challenge the Alaska Attorney General's office to do something for these exposed people. If Comp can and will produce it, I then ask them to explain what they are thinking about in ignoring this and how anyone can, even remotely, justify such catastrophic risk to innocent people.

Continuing with ideas about how to do that improving; the referee from the state, the employee and someone from the company join with this committee and are a part of it. Since the voting portion of the committee is composed of laymen, the state's officer acts as a sort of jury foreman, in that he or she helps them to both understand procedure and to recognize what they may be seeing. This officer has no vote but must participate, in the same way everyone else is instructed to do. All evidence is admissible and, if submitted, must be considered. If anything noteworthy is seen it must be brought to the attention of both the committee and the employee.

If a piece of evidence is thought to be irrelevant or obviously off base, the committee decides that by vote. The evidence is then tabled, in case something comes along that might bring it up for reconsideration. All parties are sworn to tell the truth and this is taken very seriously. Violation, if alleged, must be investigated. The hearing officer is temporarily joined by a representative from the attorney general's office for this. Confirmation of violation brings mandatory consequences. Genuine bad faith awards to the plaintiff.

To keep this from becoming of inappropriate and/or burdensome effect or even a tactic, the number of challenges can be limited to three. If two challenges turned out to be without merit, the case is closed in favor of the employer.

Material asked for must be forthcoming and, if not provided, must be accounted for. There are severe penalties for dishonesty and/or stonewalling. If either of those are found out or alleged, there must be investigation. The fact that something was not made available becomes a matter of public record. There are no statutes of limitation and violation (contempt/fraud) carries sever penalties.

If it is alleged that the unfurnished material was significant, people who might have knowledge of the subject situation are subpoenaed. Should evidence of either fraud or contempt be found, the matter is investigated and there can be consequences.

If any number of hearings are required, so be it. This can, must and will, be pursued.

All persons are advised ahead of time, in very plain wording, about procedures. Those, both the wording and the procedures, are kept as simple and straight forward as is physically possible. The key is communication and genuine understanding, all around. It is not a contest and is not allowed to become one. No one is placed at a disadvantage of any kind, in any way, shape or form. Explanations are freely given. Such is considered advisement and discussion, not "legal advice."

No person can be made or even allowed to stumble because of lack of understanding, resources, or because of manipulation. If something needs to be asked, in anyone's opinion, it is asked. Bad faith, competing or anything even close to them, by anyone, is noted, recorded and dealt with. It is an open, honest, candid and frank procedure.

Witnesses, should any be needed, are subpoenaed by the state. They serve those subpoenas, too. Hearing(s) cannot proceed until all details are in place. Telephone calls to involved people must be both recorded and documented. A summary of the messages' content has to be provided. Copies of documentation are furnished both to the employee and the assigned officer. The state's people are under strict guidelines for performance and bad faith and/or possible prejudice, there too, are both watched for and dealt with.

If agreement on a specific item is not reached it is voted on but only by the five voting members of the committee. A person can "opt out" at any time, going to the court system. If that is done, there is no "recovering of costs" to face. The case is still a Workers' Compensation Division matter. If a case does go to the courts all submitted material, having been considered or not, is admissible as evidence. If this plaintiff cannot afford or obtain counsel, one will be appointed by the state.

In the hearing, false statements in a report or before the committee are taken seriously. If falsehood is alleged it must be investigated. Objectivity must be real, not just alleged or rationalized. This should not be allowed to become a market for any medical concept, grouping or doctor. Because of its subjective nature and the jaundicing effect that can be had, if an opinion has been rendered to any such procedure by a doctor or medical group within the last six months or twice in the last two years, they are disqualified.

If something is profound; mental problems, etc, and is disagreed with, a second opinion can be requested. If that is done, the request must be honored. This opinion comes from a second professional who has not rendered an opinion within the last six months or twice in the last two years, to any such hearing.

The second opinion is really that. While it can be about a whole scenario or only address a particular portion of it, this is not a review and/or sanctioning of what someone else has come up with. Dr. Steer should never have had access to the EME report or to any other opinions from doctors who had anything to do with my case. I have heard about two doctors in my home town, who were friends, giving each other's patients "second opinions;" and of a lady, facing catastrophic surgery, who turned out to have no problem at all. That would be near to idealistic, in my opinion, compared to what I went through. All of this is paid for either by the company or their insurer.

If some profound thing, such as mental problems, is actually confirmed, the hearing officer and the committee determine the relevance of that situation toward the complaint. Even if I was as screwy as these folks alleged, I could still be harmed by the bad water at CPS and the potential for others being harmed was there, too, even if they might have been nuts. In my opinion and if I understand it, Mr. Wagg's desire to inquire about Walt's "state of mind" was interesting; possibly revealing.

Required telephonic pre-hearings explore preparations and determine witness needs, including experts. At any point agreement (Excluding the "While admitting no harm…" thing and the "This is costing too much…" one) can be reached with no down-stream sorrows for anyone, unless allegations of misconduct have been raised. This locks that part of the matter in until the allegation has been cleared up and dealt with, but the agreement process can go on. Closing of the matter by way of agreement has to be approved by the state's referee and vote of the committee, if one has been empaneled at that point, who can over-rule the referee. There are things which still must be considered, like future health risks or financial concerns, possible retaliation from an employer and identification of other potentially affected individuals.

In our improved Workers' Compensation Division scenario there can be no assuming that people are not affected because they do not "come forward." There should be no company rule allowed or government law made, which says that a person must come forward, either, because of the very real world risk of falling into disfavor with an employer or an insensitive world. Good faith should never be assumed. It must be demonstrated by honest cooperation and failure to do that should bring hefty consequences.

Each item of the hearing would be cleared by mutual agreement of the parties (best option) or by vote of the five voting members of the committee. This last part is semi-final because positions can change as the process continues. The hearing statement would be written as items are disposed of and/or modified, if it was thought to be advisable, by (1) mutual agreement or (2) vote of the five person committee. A required final round, announced as such, recaps each decision, secures confirmations and solidifies the hearing statement. During that round anything can be addressed, revisited or modified. A "final round" might be approached and re-approached, before one is secured.

Verdicts would evolve in hearing and be mutually agreed upon, item by item, by the end of the meeting or meetings. A part of this would be to determine what harm has actually been done, what future problems or difficulties might present themselves, (etc.). It is over when everyone feels, or the voting members of the committee say, that it is over.

It may be that a lot of this could be handled in the way I originally thought it was being handled; by submitting information and talking about it. It might not even be necessary to set up a formal hearing.

The overseeing officer recommends settlement based on formulas arrived at by a legislative panel. Those recommendations are voted on by the five member committee, with their majority vote prevailing. Settlements ought to include realistic punitive damages where they apply. Those help to keep honest people honest. They keep the world (and victims) from having to bow to – or to be deceived by – lies, rationalization or whims. Along with all of it, there should be serious penalties for problems where there is turpitude. Being determinedly one-sided can be seen as aligning with, or contributing to, turpitude.

It seems to be an informative thing that a plant foreman had to be told, week after week, twice, about an increasing problem that was as close as the water cooler. He would not hear it or even humor people by taking a drink. Probably interesting too is that, even at the end of the second time around, it took a certain person to get him to even try it. If a member of the operations crew had complained again that morning, it wouldn't have happened. I speak advisedly, from what I had both seen with my own eyes and heard with my own ears, for weeks—twice. All of this was about a water system which was known to have had contamination problems in the past.

We top all of this off in noting that he still didn't believe it, years later, in spite of the fact that he recorded the situations in detail, twice. It was Jay, who ordered the repair both times. Our alternates were as bad or worse. Not a glimmer or a peep. I suppose that no one on their crew drank the water at all or very, very little of it. That idea is not far-fetched, in spite of the fact that we were all working twelve hour shifts. It was their leader, Curley, though, who came to the plant to tell me I had "made a lot of big guys mad," at the camp.

Given some people's willingness to hold a grudge there are a few last thoughts, here. If the employee prevails or not, and goes back to work, it would take state approval to fire him or to lay him off. Charges that he was being a pain in the neck, though, would be taken seriously. Claims that an employer was, or other employees were, harassing someone would be taken seriously, too. If the employer desired for settlement to include the employee's separation, this could be a part of what is arrived at but must be approved by the state's man, the committee and the employee.

Win, lose or settled early on, having had a contested Workers' Compensation Division case should not be information which is accessible to anyone outside the government, in any context or through any mechanism. One of my sons is a computer buff. He said that he once typed in his name, which is the same as mine, and hit the button. To his surprise, the screen began to fill up. There were details of my case surrounding the fact that I had charged the company with fraud. These folks said they had no way of addressing such a charge and described their program as "beneficent."

Chapter Thirty-One
Life Goes On

One retired fellow said that he hoped I would eventually get a shot at "the good life." I don't need to go south for the winter or to go on cruises but it would be great not to have to worry so much. That man was a retired executive from Burlington Northern Railroad. He had some interesting things to say to me but I think his comments should raise eye-brows for everyone. The quote offered here is near verbatim. "We (the railroads) missed our chance to get into Workers' Compensation. We could have gotten into it but had our own system and were doing things our own way, using company people and lawyers. By the time we saw the mistake it was too late. Our costs of addressing the legal aspects of employees' problems have risen while Workers' Compensation Division's people have been able to hold the line."

Remembering what my aunt said about the people at Union Pacific; "I don't know why they don't have the same ethics as the rest of us do, but they don't." If people like that are losing ground, while the folks at Workers' Compensation Division are "holding the line," we can only wonder...

By 1999 a lot of time had gone by. It seemed at times, with me, that the "lights were on but nobody was home," as they say. There were two car wrecks, about six months apart. Each time, the world seemed to be clearly seen and firmly in control. I was just going down the road knowing where I was and what was going on. It turned out that neither was the case. Proof of that, the second time, turned out to be an intersection with a red light in it and the side of a fellow's van. Failure to recognize my son in law in his own home, where I had been visiting, was of concern to my daughter, too. They had been married for ten years and were the parents of four of my grandchildren.

I went to a warehouse with a fellow I was doing some work for. We stopped in the parking lot and walked into the building. I had never been there before and no one else was around. Inside, were vehicles, some equipment and a storage area. I was given a box of power staples and told to put them in the van. A white one, it was parked where we had left it a few minutes before. I clearly remember putting the staples under the front of my seat, where they would be easy to get to but not in the way of my feet.

The whole warehouse experience was about ten minutes long. In leaving, I felt confusion. Somehow, the fact that there was more in life than the inside of this building had escaped me. The door was a new idea and I felt turned around. When that door was opened a strange looking, unfamiliar and rather hostile feeling world was seen. A stark and harsh-seeming yellow glow (sunlight) shone on a strange looking and quite unfamiliar white van, which seemed to resemble a toy one. The word Tonka actually flashed in my mind. I felt slightly off balance and mildly sick. Inside me, it seemed as if my head—or my awareness—was turned slightly to the left. The experience lasted for only a moment and memory of it evaporated.

We got into the van and went to our job. Jumping out, I reached under the seat for those staples. They weren't there. The other man thought I might have left them in the warehouse but my memory was too clear. They should have been under the front of the seat. Later in the day, suddenly and for no understandable reason, I heard myself say "If you can't find those staples, you might look in the van that's in the warehouse." It was a blue one that I had never seen before and didn't even remember being there, until this just slipped out. As it was said memory returned, of what had happened during leaving the building.

I had to get some help and wondered where money was going to come from to pay for it. A doctor friend told me, quietly, that I should probably say nothing about the water. The new man seemed interested. He told me that it looked as if I had suffered a head injury at one time. There would be some testing. He said medical advancements had been made in the last few years.

What was happening seems to be related to Dr. Weldon's comments about the "Alzheimer-like condition." Regular reviews of my situation, like the ones he recommended, might have detected growing concerns. He said that cognitive problems would probably endure for my lifetime. The diarrhea and rash went away very suddenly, years ago. Some other things moderated and even went away, too. I had thought that these cognitive problems were getting better. My wife would say "You're not the man you were" and "You're not right, yet." Apparently she was noticing something that I wasn't able to see.

I was away from home at the time of that second accident. My daughter called her mom to tell about it. She told me that my wife said "Someday he's going to kill someone and then maybe people will listen to me."

(September 11, 2006) I saw the doctor about my PET scan. The thing in my lungs is benign. The breathing test that was done shows a problem but it seems to respond to medicating. We talked about the problems and I said I knew what had caused them. The man who had been so strict about not being told "one word" about industrial exposure had the slightest hint of a smile I have ever seen.

The cognitive testing done in 1999 was with another doctor, who did essentially the same interview and test as Doctor Thorner had done in Seattle and Dr. Craig did in Anchorage. This new examiner seems to have had quite a different impression of me than either of them. She knew nothing of the water. Testing results came in; Pre-senile Dementia. The initial doctor commented that I was very young for this. He told me it would probably get worse. This man said he was concerned for me, of course, but he was more worried about other drivers. I wondered how I'm supposed to make a living without driving. Most of what I do involves looking for work, getting to and from it and hauling tools and supplies. Also affecting work is making simple mistakes and looking for tools all day, sometimes almost tripping over them while that's going on. When this happens I feel frustrated and panicky.

I was taking medication, early on. The doctor had said this stuff would take awhile before improvement was noticeable. One day, driving along, I happened to notice the scenery, which was pretty. There were hills, trees and a stop sign. The sign raised no recognition at all. That came with my wife yelling "aren't you going to stop?" Things did seem to get better, though.

Around ten years into the medications (2008) I took a bottle of milk from the fridge, removed the plastic seal and put it into the trash. Then, doing something (?) around the kitchen, I recall thinking that I needed to put some milk on my cereal but couldn't find it. That increasing panic was felt. I looked all over the house, wondering where I might have been and put the milk down. Finally and absently, I looked into the refrigerator. The milk was setting there with its seal still in place. I hadn't touched it. It was then that realization came. I hadn't been taking my medication. Then, too, I remembered two times during the last week when cars had come out of nowhere and there had been close calls. One of those was when I was taking my granddaughter to school. I bought a little plastic thing that people who take pills use. It has compartments marked for each day of the week and has helped.

Several years ago, before the hearing, a good job came up on a construction project. I really wanted it and filled out an application. The very first question was if I had ever had a Workers' Compensation (L&I) claim. I felt sick and almost went home but stayed and filled out the form. The next part of the hiring process was examination by a doctor, who asked what the "Comp case" was about. This person listened and then said "bummer." I found out, quietly, that these things are known. I got the job and it was great. For construction this was a good one too, at prevailing wage, and lasted for almost three months. That was different from the "You are here for as long as you want to be" type of work that I was used to but it was badly needed and very welcome.

One of my daughters knows a man who works in the Risk Management department of a big company. She told him about my situation. He said there will never be anything I can do about it.

In 2000 I got word that one of our guys had died of cancer. In a few months another one of our people was flown into Anchorage, with cancer. A picture came into my mind. I was aware of two more of our guys who were cancer victims. That filter and those coffee grounds may have helped people to escape some things but that was probably not nearly good enough. Early on, in 1993, I had written about what I suspected. This was that our crew would eventually have a higher than usual rate of cancer. That does seem to be coming true. To me, it's not only unfortunate but very tragic.

I wrote to BP's big guy in Alaska, with copies to Jay and the governor, telling them what I thought about these things. Also told them, was about the list I had submitted, asking for our people to be identified and monitored for their protection. My concern is about both cancer and potential cognitive problems (and, perhaps, heart problems) but I only wrote about the cancer.

I believe exposed people should have been identified and monitored. Whatever a person might think about my story, there are facts. One of those facts is that they were not monitored. Another fact is that the list of them submitted and resubmitted to the state has never even been acknowledged. It includes people who, I am convinced, have died because of the situation.

When I wrote to Governor Knowles, he asked Mr. Grossi to answer for him. Grossi informed me that my Workers' Compensation case was long over and that the time for appeals was past. He cited my "day long hearing" (about five hours including the break for lunch) as if it was something that made sense. A later letter to Governor Knowles was answered by a man that I knew; Chuck Mahlen, who had become commissioner of Labor. He told me that these laws had been passed to take a load off the court-system. The next try drew an answer from a Mr. Flannagan. He said that Mr. Grossi had once told him I had alleged wrong-doing during my case and that if I wasn't satisfied I should have gone to the court system.

When Fred died I did quite a bit of calling around. Mr. Jaquot declined to speak to me. Ms. Gaal had retired. One of the things learned was that Mr. Grossi seems to have gravitated in the Workers' Compensation Division. I was told that he was in charge of their fraud operations. Another person in Anchorage told me I should go to the Attorney General. I commented about how futile that had been and was told there was a new attorney general now. It seems that, in his practice, he had represented injured workers. I wrote and sent a manuscript copy of this material. A letter came right back, thanking me for the material and saying it had been forwarded to OSHA.

When I sent my material to the Attorney General's office I also sent it to B.P.'s vice president, in Anchorage. His reply said the matter had been investigated and was closed. If I had new information, he said, they would be glad to consider it. Mr. Suttles assured me that my manuscript had been read. I wrote back, saying if he would read it he might not be willing to say such a thing (that there had actually been an investigation). His answer informed me that they were aware of my documentation, naming it all.

No offense is intended to anyone and no harm is intended. I really do not have any bad feelings or animosity toward anyone. If I can lose everything; my job, career, reputation, home, health and retirement; if I can be certified to have mental problems and go through all of this, struggling just to make a living as an older person who has lost access to the field of his training and experience, I might be extended some patience.

What happened with the potable water system at CPS was a blunder; pure and simple. What happened after that was not even close to right. I am not aware of any of our people that have died, who had not had cancer. During a trip through another state, in a tiny town, I asked a man who owned a store if he knew a local fellow who had been one of our crew-members. He said yes and that this had been a swell guy. Then he spoke of the death and of what became of the family after that.

Somewhere, somebody must care. I want for our people to be identified and monitored while some of them are still alive. To me, that doesn't seem to be asking too much.

www.ingramcontent.com/pod-product-compliance
Lightning Source LLC
LaVergne TN
LVHW021505080426
835509LV00018B/2406